A Big Dick and Bald Head Ain't Worth the Hassle

SISTA E

Copyright © 2022 Sista E
All rights reserved
First Edition

Fulton Books
Meadville, PA

Published by Fulton Books 2022

ISBN 978-1-63860-136-4 (paperback)
ISBN 978-1-63860-137-1 (digital)

Printed in the United States of America

CONTENTS

Foreword v
Introduction vii

Momma, May I? 1
Run, Girl, Run 9
Soul Mate 15
Hypothetically Speaking 32
The Bus Ride 45
Oatmeal Cookies and Me 69
So, You're Pregnant. Now What? 96
In Love with Lust 115
When Loving You Is Hurting Me 162
Between You and Me 175
Clark Kent *is* Superman 188
Exhale Him, Inhale You, Breathe 206
Heal With Courage, Strength, & Wisdom 214
Finish Strong: Sing, Sing, Celebrate 218
Love Tokens 223
Closing Prayer 225

FOREWORD

By Cocoa "One Funny Momma" Brown

When I first saw the title of this book, the scream I let out could've been heard across four states. As a 40 none of ya business year old woman, I have lived and dated through a lot of eras; the break-dancer phase, the new jack swing phase, the pretty boy phase and finally, the Dark Vader phase. But it's something about them bald heads and big ole…feet, that'll have you acting a plum fool! I can't lie, for many years that combination had me half Stevie Wonder and half Radio; blind and special. For so long I thought God made these types of men to be our kryptonite, like there was nothing you could do to not fall under their spell. But as I got older and wiser, I realized that they weren't some magical being that practice voodoo mixed with amazing sex. I realized it was something in me that kept attracting these emotionally unavailable men that ran game like drinking water. I think the hardest but best thing we as women who keep attracting men that break our backs and our hearts can do is have that "Come to Jesus moment", and instead of pointing the finger at him or them, turning that finger around and going deep inside the woman we are, or the woman we portray to be or maybe the woman we are running away from becoming. Finally, a book comes along that lets me and other women and hey some men too, know that they are not alone when it comes to the falling for the banana in the tailpipe (all pun intended). But with some self-reflection and hard knock honesty, we can all be "hassle" free, unless we want to be "hassled".

INTRODUCTION

I am a storyteller, evangelist, and certified life coach writing an inspirational self-help book for women. While reading this book, my hope is that you will laugh, cry, and *think*. And in the end, you'll be motivated to move and heal.

In this book, you'll find true stories of the men my soul was drawn to because I never healed from the initial hurt. You'll see that a broken-smiled little girl turned into a chaotic, destructive, bitter, hateful, vengeful woman, grown by age and looks but still a little girl by action—yes, an angry woman.

Many women go through life with unresolved hurt from previous relationships, whether from a relationship with your father or your mate. And we carry that hurt for many years after the incident. All women do, even the church-going women.

Now, some may mask it, and some may attempt to hide it. It doesn't matter if they're young or old. The hurt is real, and many times it lingers. It's the lingering that causes the hurt woman to hurt others.

Our hurt from past relationships flows into our lives and rubs off on our children, onto our next relationship, and sometimes into the next generation—the grief, the pain, the remembering of yesterdays. Often, we use sex as a means to heal or a means to cope when, in reality, sex turns unresolved and unsolved into pain. And that makes everything worse.

Now, this book is not a man-hating, male-bashing, let's-talk-bad-about-men book. Instead, this is about women owning their part in the hurt and breakdown of the relationship.

Inside this book, you'll read stories about my life, love, and mistakes thereof. But also, sound advice for healing and better living.

We can grow through what we are going through and heal at the same time.

Sometimes it's in the looking-back that we fall down when we really need a step-by-step action plan to heal.

Many church folks say you need to get over this or that but never give you actionable steps to execute that healing process and release strongholds.

Let's talk about it, but then let's put it into action to heal the hearts and minds of the broken. We are called by God to be doers of the word. This book breaks down an action plan for healing results.

We want to take women from bitter to better, from broken to healed. We'll discuss how to recover from the brokenness, then how to get over it. Whatever it may be, there's a process to healing, and this book shows you how.

Many will be offended by my title. Oh, such vulgar language from a lady. I can hear my momma singing that song, "Girls can't do what the guys do and still be a lady." I say, "Okay, what should we say?" Because truly *dick* is slang for penis. And they both mean heartbreak—well, in this story anyway.

Now, if you need the *Webster's Dictionary* definition of politically correct—sweet, not spicy with everything nice—then, baby, this ain't the book for you. This book is all about truth—my truth and nothing but my truth. But hey, in the words of Adele, "I'm such an f'n lady!"

Introduction

Sidenote: Names have been changed to protect the identity of these lairs, hoes, and haters to keep me from completely jumping on their heads and blowing up their true identities.

And as I said above, in case you were wondering, this is not a male-bashing book. I love the fellas. We need our men. This book is about accountability and healing.

Sista Girl, we have to accept that we played our part in it. Let's laugh, cry, and heal together. This book is about lessons learned and how to move from pain to purpose. It's also about learning the difference between love and lust. Let's move from broken and bitter to beautiful and blossoming.

One famous songwriter said, "We fall down, but we get up." This book gives you the steps to get back up. We have all been there a time or two, some more than others. Yes, you want to cry. Yes, it hurt, but now it's time to dry those eyes and get up. And here's how.

Shall we begin?

Yes, we shall!

CHAPTER 1

Momma, May I?

I was once asked a question by this guy. "How can I be a good man to a woman who enjoys being a man?" I laughed. I knew exactly where he was coming from, and it had nothing to do with sexuality but everything to do with femininity.

We, the women of Generation X, were raised with this old saying that goes, "We love our sons, but we raise our daughters." Yup, the baby-boomer women were so strong and wanted independence so much they fed it to their daughters. They rejected and redefined tradition. And now their daughters are so strong and independent that they've become too manly for a man.

Keep in mind that with the same thought process, those same mothers loved their sons, spoiled them, nurtured them to be carefree, and forgot to raise them. They forgot to put the same spice into their sons that they put into their daughters. Now you have these metrosexual and half-baked men going from bed to bed, woman to woman, mama to mommy, looking for the mothering validation.

This brings me to Mr. Momma's Boy. Now here is where I want to scream. In fact, give me a second because *I am* about to scream. Ahhh!

Momma, he ain't yo husband, nor is he your child. He's your *son*, your grow-ass son, and that makes a difference. If he's over eighteen, sticking his thang in this one and that one, passing it out through the neighborhoods like its candy, he, my dear, is community dick. And, Momma, he ain't a child! It's time you let him grow up—man up if you will.

Come on now. By the age of twenty-five, definitely thirty, if you don't see your son out there soaring, give him a push, a boost, but not yo titties to hang on to.

Okay, okay. Now that I got that out, I'm back.

I once dated a guy who lived with his momma. Now there's a difference between living with your mom so you can take care of her and living with her because you don't want to leave the nest or *can't* leave the nest. This momma had a husband and still treated her son better than her spouse. And she didn't like me. In her mind, I was the other woman. In my mind, I was like, Look, lady. If he's doing the same things he does to me to you, then we have a problem. But she really didn't like me; she treated me like I was the mistress.

Oh, they ate dinner together and went grocery shopping together. They talked politics, they gossiped about family, and they discussed bills. She told him how to take care of his kids, when to shower, where to go—she did everything! And he allowed it.

I soon learned there would never be room enough in his life for me and her. She went as far as to tell me, "Emori, you will never have him to yourself."

Now, what was I to do with a statement like that? I couldn't fight him on it; that was his mother. Whatever he needed or wanted came from her except, well, you know. And that's all I was good for.

I tried explaining to him that this wasn't a normal mother-and-son relationship. I tried explaining about boundaries. But nope, I was the problem. He thought I was jealous.

How do you compete with a man's mother? She had been there by his side and had done everything for him. She cooked, he ate. Whenever she called his name, he jumped. He needed a place to rest, and she gave him a home. Something needed fixing, she called him. It was like watching an old married couple, but I was looking at a mother and her son.

They fought but made right up. He could do no wrong in her eyes unless he didn't do what she wanted him to do, which was a rare occasion.

Now I get it, this was a broken man. Although he was over forty, his mother was still the leading lady in his world. He had commitment issues, he had financial issues, and he had issues—major issues, not problems. Problems can be solved. But Sis, this dude had issues. He needed to lie on a couch. But instead, he lied to me.

I saw all the signs. I even fought to get his attention. I pulled out all the stops. I wined and dined him. One time I even set up a romantic evening that included a roll in the hay afterward. Well, that roll in the hay consisted of some heads banging, legs swinging, sweating my newly bought hairdo out. And no condoms.

Why no condoms? Because I was convinced, he was mine and I was his. He loved me, and I was in love with him. I mean, we were soon to be married; well, in my mind, we were.

But later, I found out some other woman had just done the exact same thing I did, only a month earlier.

It was his fortieth birthday. He had just lost his favorite auntie, and I wanted to cheer him up. I rented a hotel room. I bought him this exquisite watch. You know, like B said, "Let me upgrade you." So, I was trying to upgrade him. All the while, he was degrading me.

I rented a private yacht, and we went out on the ocean. My hair was blowing in the wind. I was in heaven. Life couldn't get any better than this. I knew I was looking good. I had my DKNY white wedges on, my white linen short shorts, and my multicolored A-lined shirt. My fingernails and toes were suck-a-boo ready, and my hair was fierce and flowing.

He's kissing me on my neck and lips in public, rubbing all over me. You know, the foreplay before we play.

We got back to the hotel room, where I had rose petals leading from the door to the bed and more of his favorite drink—gin makes him sin. I changed into something more comfortable; well, it was my birthday suit for his birthday. And oh, the party escalated.

I exhaled, swerving on that surfboard, I was falling more in love and in love and in love. As we switched places, he threw my legs apart, one to the east and one to the west, and he entered in between to do his best. I cried and cried because the day had been such a perfect day, and I didn't want it to end. Yeah, well, reality would soon set in.

He was up and out the door before long because, you guessed it, Mommy Dearest called.

I rolled over to go to sleep, but before I did, I grabbed my phone and looked at *fake* book. Why Lawd, did I go on Facebook?

I went to his page, and something told me to look through his pictures. Well, I was so in love with this man that I just needed to see more of him, right? Wrong!

I saw a tagged picture of him with this chick, this ugly chick at that, and he's holding her. Nah, bruh, this was no sisterly hug.

As I was looking, I saw water and boats, and familiarity set in. *Hey, wait a minute, this looks like the exact same pier we were just on.* I thought to myself, *No, this can't be the same. It has to be a different pier.* Nope, it wasn't.

Turns out she had taken him there just the month before, and I was clueless. So here I thought I was doing something amazing—dinner on a yacht as we sailed the ocean. No. She had done the exact same before me.

Now I was upset, in disbelief, angry as ever. So, I called him. He was like, "That picture is old. Why are you bringing that up? I told you it was over with her."

"I just want you to tell me it's not the same pier, the same yacht, the same boat, the same idea."

Would you believe this dude got upset?

I hung up the phone and turned my ringer off. I needed time to myself, to soak in how stupid I had just been and all the money I had just spent and all the time and energy I had just put in.

I walked downstairs to the bar—remember I'm still at the hotel, *by myself*—to grab some wine and just clear my head.

You know, when you start to measure how stupid you are versus how well this other chick looks compared to you? When you begin to think why-her-and-not-me thoughts?

Yes, that's where I was mentally while sipping my glass of pomegranate wine. It was good too.

So, there I was enjoying my drink and the vibes, just relaxing and unwinding, and this dude comes barging in the hotel, swole like he owns the place, huffing and puffing. I saw him almost immediately, although it took him a minute to see me. When he did, he came right over and demanded that I get up and come with him.

I told him, "No, I'm enjoying my glass."

He snatched it from my fingers and dragged me out the door.

Now, folks were looking at me like I was crazy as this dude was yelling and pulling on me. We got outside, and he continues yelling, trying to get his point across. He wanted me to believe it wasn't the same place. I just wanted to enjoy my drink, so I tried to go back inside. But he kept on grabbing and dragging me.

I said, "Let me go."

This dude slapped me and said, "Listen!"

Now at this point, all I heard was Charlie Brown's "Wah, wa, wa, wah, wa, wa." I heard nothing. I was too busy weighing my options. Was I about to play the victim or be that bitch?

I quickly lowered my voice, sobered up, and said slowly, "Let…me…go!" It was definitely a Dr. Jekyll–Mr. Hyde moment for me. I couldn't believe this man had just slapped me for calling him on his bull.

But I loved this man. Yeah, okay. But he forgot to love me back.

In that moment, I remembered love is a verb, and his actions tonight with that one slap had me realizing it wasn't love but lust. He had just dicked me down so much that I became blind to his many flaws. And, Sista Girl, trust me, his flaws were plenty and many.

Now, who was wrong? Was I wrong for trying to cheer him up, for trying to change him, trying to upgrade him, trying to be his everything? Or was he wrong for not making me his everything and changing?

Yes, no doubt he was wrong for slapping me. Had it not been for the grace of God, that one slap could have gone a whole different way. That slap could have landed someone in jail and the other in the hospital, and it could have easily gone either way.

I'm that chick. I often warn people that I may have moved to the suburbs, but I ain't from there. But that's another book. I'm like Miss Celie. I have been fighting fools all my life. But remember now, less than two hours before this revelation, he was in between my legs, giving me the best that he's got.

How was that not a clue? The best thing that he's got was between his legs. This man had nothing to offer me. He was attached to his mother. He was the worst case of mama's boy I had ever experienced in my entire life. Neither he nor his mother knew boundaries.

So, what do you think happened next?

Someone in the hotel had called the police. The police came, and I lied. "There's no problem here, Officer. All is well." Of course, the officer wanted to take names and ask questions. We just stood there, answering and lying while looking at each other, all stupid.

The officers—there were two of them—let us leave and told Mr. Mama's Boy to drive off as I went inside the hotel.

I got to my room, and my phone was just blowing up from all of his calls and text messages. Yup, he apologized profusely. And what did I do? I answered the phone and let him come back over to apologize in person. I let him sweet-talk me into flopping my legs right back open. That had to have been the best dick he had ever given me, or was it?

Was I just blinded by the dick? Ladies, a big dick and a bald head—is it worth the hassle?

We begin to allow men to slide on the very things we say we wouldn't allow. We say, "Oh, girl, I wouldn't take that if I were you." Yes, remember saying that to a friend or about a friend?

This is why it's so important not to sleep with the man before you're clear on who he is and clear on who you are.

As women, we give away crowns to a clown and all in the name of love when, in fact, he didn't earn the title of a king that we were so quick to give.

> Why do we fall in love so easily without him ever earning our love, respect, and trust? Is it because we're longing for daddy's love, or are we just longing for that TV love? You know the love you see given in a scripted scene, created out of someone's fancy?

How did I get here? How did I end up involved with a momma's boy? I was captain of my soul, master of my destiny. I knew who I was and *whose* I was. I was a confident woman who knew what she wanted out of life, and I was clear on where my life was headed—or so I thought, or so I felt.

So, let me tell you how a confident, determined, strong-willed woman got to be involved so heavily with a momma's boy. Let's go back to when I left my momma's house and went off for college. I mean, after all, my momma sent me to college to get a husband, not just an education.

CHAPTER 2

Run, Girl, Run

I had graduated from high school in June the prior year, and according to my mother's dreams, I was to leave immediately for college.

> How many people know college isn't for everyone? Sometimes you have to consider trade schools or technical schools... But let's get back to my story.

I had been through the high school love sagas of dating the popular boys and the bad boys and the drug dealers and gangbangers, all in hopes of rebelling against my parents until that bad-boy, drug dealer, gangbanger boyfriend kidnapped me and held me hostage in Robert Taylor Homes.

Robert Taylor Homes—according to *Wikipedia*—was a public housing project in the Bronzeville neighborhood on the South Side of Chicago, Illinois. According to folks who lived in or around Chicago, Illinois, Robert Taylor Homes was the second most dangerous place in Chicago you could ever go. And I was there for a few days unable to leave.

You needed a key to get in and out the front door. And outsiders weren't welcomed through the apartment's gates. However, I was invited in. I thought I was hanging with my boyfriend, defining all things my momma taught me. I thought I was big and bad and could handle anything on my own at eighteen years old.

Besides, this wasn't the first gangbanger boyfriend I had. No, he wasn't, but he was the first *killer* boyfriend I had.

Of course, I didn't know he was a killer, but would soon learn that and not the easy way.

Leon was a notorious gang member in Chicago, Illinois, who fled Chicago to come to Milwaukee, Wisconsin, because the streets had gotten too hot for him on the South Side.

A lot of people would come from Chicago to Milwaukee because the welfare system in Milwaukee gave out more money and more food stamps. Milwaukee was about an hour-and-a-half drive away. That made it easy for a lot of people to compute between the two cities.

My then-boyfriend asked me to take a trip with him back to Chicago. He said we're going to go and come right back. Leon said he just wanted me to ride along because he wanted his girl with him. Little did I know Leon had just committed a murder in Milwaukee and needed to leave.

I, being the most rebellious teenager in the world, said, "Sure, let's go," and rode with him and a few of his family members and friends back to Chicago.

Now, I had heard the stories of their life in Chicago, stories about them selling drugs and living in the projects. In contrast, I was a little PK—preacher's kid, in case you don't know—who had grown up attending church three times a week and twice on Sundays. I was also a little Prezi girl who went to an all-girls private school throughout high school. A little girl with two working parents who lived in decent neighborhoods and never lived in the projects. Admittedly, I was a spoiled little girl who always lived in a house, never an apartment. And Little Ms. Know-It-All thought taking this trip with Leon would be fun.

I glamorized being with a drug dealer gangbanger because I thought it was cute or fun; it was not what I knew growing up. Besides, I knew this man loved me and would always take care of me. Yup, at eighteen, I knew it all and I was grown. Right?

I decided to leave the safety of my momma's bosoms for some dick. Let's just say what it was. It was dick. This little girl got her first taste of grown-man dick. He was several years older than me—seven to be exact. And I knew I was in love. He wasn't just sticking his finger in my pussy. He wasn't just sucking on my breast. He loved me. He brought me food, and he penetrated my soul.

I had too much responsibility at my momma's house, but this man was taking care of me. He said we would always be together. Little did I know he meant until death parted us.

This man got me to Chicago, and we ended up having to stay overnight and then another night, and now it was night three, and I was ready to go on day one. Honestly, I was ready to go about ten minutes after I got there. I became scared, and I hadn't called home.

I saw him get high off his own supply, and Leon soon became violent toward me. He kept me locked up in this apartment in Robert Taylor, and because I was an outsider, I couldn't just go out the door by myself without something dangerous happening to me.

By the third night, I asked to go to the store for some snacks. He allowed me to go but only with his cousin as my escort. While she wasn't looking, I grabbed the payphone and called my biological daddy. I told him I was in Chicago, stuck and really needed to get home. I asked him to send me some money to get home.

He said, "You got there. Now get yourself home" and hung up on me. It was the single most devastating thing I had experienced. My heart just broke right there at that Shell gas station. On my one phone call, I called my daddy in St. Louis to help get me home, and he rejected me. Now, I really felt trapped. I believed all hope was lost and that I would never get home back to Milwaukee.

> How many of you know there is a daddy who will never turn his back on you no matter how bad you've messed up? Thankfully, my daddy up in heaven had my back; the Father up above had me covered. It was the prayers of my momma and my grandma, who had prayed and the angels sent before me to protected me.

Just as we were on our way back into Robert Taylor Homes, Leon's brother came rushing in. He was my BFF Ron Ron's boyfriend. Yup, we dated brothers.

So, Leon's brother comes and grabs my arm and says, "Look, come with me."

The cousin was like, "All right, y'all, I'll see y'all when you get upstairs." Lucky for me, she was high as a kite.

I went with the brother. I didn't have a clue where we were going, but it wasn't toward the inside of that apartment, and I was okay with that. He was walking fast and pulling me along. As we got closer to the outside of Robert Taylor Homes, he said, "You're

Run, Girl, Run

going home. Don't ask no questions. Just go." He threw me in this car, and I looked up and saw it was my momma and my other best friend, Trese inside, and we drove off quickly.

It was a quiet ride home. My momma didn't ask any questions, and I couldn't speak. Tears began to flow down my face. I felt pure shame. But at the same time, I was just so happy to be going home and safe with my momma.

Soon after that, Leon got arrested for murder, and I restarted beauty school. The murder charges stuck, and Leon regularly made calls to me saying stuff like, "If I can't have you, nobody will. You will always be mine."

But now that he was locked up, I thought he couldn't get to me. I thought, "Oh, he's locked up, and I can move on with my life." Nope. He would call wherever I was. He became obsessed with me. He had already stalked me in the prior months when we had broken up once or twice before. Now he was stalking me from jail.

Eventually, I became weary. I went to my momma and said, "Okay, I'm ready to leave for college now." After a big Christmas at home with my family, including my granny, I left Milwaukee, Wisconsin, and landed in Atlanta, Georgia, heading to the campus of Morris Brown College.

I left a big city, my big family, and moved onto the campus where I was responsible for no one but me. I went from being the oldest girl to just a girl. My life would now begin. I was free of gangs and free of drugs. I was free of my momma and raising her kids, and I was free from the rejection from my biological father. I was free from this stalker ex-boyfriend and free from working at Burger King and getting robbed. I was free of gunfire, and I was free from being the preacher's kid. No one here knew me, and I wasn't responsible for anyone but me.

It was a whole new world. The people here looked like me and didn't need me, but I needed them. They were doing better, living better, and it wasn't because of drugs. It was because of education.

My mind would quickly adapt to my new surroundings. I would adjust to college life, this new life in another state, with no guns or drugs—well, not the same drugs.

I was off to live a new life of just being a college student, not a drug dealer's girl, and not a gangbanger's girl. Not the evangelist's daughter, the bishop's daughter, and not the big sister momma. I was just a college kid from Milwaukee.

CHAPTER 3

Soul Mate

We ladies fall in love so quickly and so fast that men don't even have to earn it most times. All they have to do is give us good dick. Once he does, and we make that sound, we accept all his baggage and bull spit. When the truth is, once we start to love ourselves, anything less than love becomes non-negotiable.

The problem is daddy wasn't in our lives or was part-time in our lives, so we don't know what love from a man looks like. We take the smallest thing and equate that to love.

But take a pause here. An orgasm, a good old-fashioned shaken-from-your-head-to-your-toes, got-you-calling-for-Jesus-or-your-momma orgasm is not love. Just because he made you feel good doesn't mean he loves you. It simply means he wet your pussy, *well*. And if you know like I know, a well-wet pussy ain't paying no light bills.

Here's what I've learned over the years with big dicks and bald heads. Now, don't get me wrong, the little dicks aren't worth it either, but they're not worth talking about because we usually get rid of the little-dick boys quickly because they can't scratch the surface and make you make that sound. You know that sound? The one where you spend your life savings to prove to this man that you're the one or we do things that you know your momma taught you better than to do. You know, when we get on our knees, but it's not to pray, it's to play.

Soul mates. Our soul mate is made just for us sent by God. We're looking for that one to connect to our body and our soul.

> How many of you know that the devil knows exactly what you like? He knows exactly what you need. Sometimes he knows better than you do, which is why he sends temptation our way. Just to throw us off from our destiny.

I met my soul mate while I was in college. He worked at the school while I attended. Yep, that was called fraternization. Fraternization is defined as "a relationship that falls outside of normal school-related interactions and communications, which is usually—but not necessarily—romantic or sexual." In basic terms, it means if you work for the school, you cannot date or have sex with a student who attends the college that pays your bills.

Yep, we defiled that at the very beginning.

It's funny how your name can precede you. Some of the officers at my school knew who I was before I ever knew they existed.

It was the fall semester. I had just gotten back to Morris Brown College Campus to begin a new semester. I was starting my junior year, and I had my first car. I was looking good, smelling good, feeling good. You couldn't tell me nothing.

My car was a white Camry with personalized Wisconsin tags that read "MZE2U." Personalized tags were the thing back then. It made a statement about the owner. You got to say it with your chest except it was in seven letters or less and on your license plates. My tags signified cockiness and arrogance, and I was all of the above at the time.

My confidence was extremely high. I was young with no kids, little money, and in college. It didn't hurt that I was cute too.

I was independent and free. I had gentlemen callers regularly. I had students and a few professors. I had no regard for anyone or anything but what I wanted. That was until love stuck its head in my business and caught me up like a gazelle caught in a lion's mouth.

I was driving down the street passing the Middleton Complex, the Towers, which were the dormitories at Morris Brown. It had just started to get dark. I made a left turn and then turned into the gym's parking lot, as that's where I was headed. It wasn't until then that I noticed the lights from a campus police car.

I opened my door to get out, but the officer said over his speaker, "Stay in the car, please."

I looked around and didn't see anyone else, so I said to myself, "I guess he's talking to me."

The officer approached my car, and of course, I now had a full-blown attitude. He said, "Ma'am, why didn't you stop when you saw the police lights or heard the siren?"

With my head tilted, I replied, "I didn't know you were pulling me over. Besides, what do you want with me anyway?"

"May I have your license and registration."

"You may not. Why are you pulling me over is the first topic for discussion."

"Well, you don't have any good tags on your car."

"If I'm not mistaken, it has drive-off tags that have not yet expired."

"They expire tomorrow."

"Well, then let's have this conversation tomorrow when they do expire." My tags were in the window. I had just gotten them but had not had the chance to put them on my car.

Sista E

The officer said, "Well, I need to see your insurance along with your license and registration."

"Until or unless you give me a valid reason for holding me up, I'm not showing you anything."

He returned to his car and got on his radio. When he came back, I asked again, "Sir, why did you stop me?"

"You ran the stop sign and then didn't pull over with the siren and lights."

Inside, I rolled my eyes. "Fine, here's my license and registration."

After he looked it all over, he said, "This all says 'Wisconsin.'"

"Hello. Because that's where I'm from."

"How long have you been in Georgia?"

"Two years."

"Well, legally, you have thirty days to update your information."

"Wrong again. I'm a college student, and my permanent residence is in Wisconsin. I don't have to change anything."

"Ma'am, I'm going to ask you for your insurance one more time."

"Look, Mr. Flashlight Cop, I have places to be. I don't have time for this."

His mouth tightened. "Ma'am, you're not going anywhere but to jail." That's when another officer's car approached, and by then, my little smart-mouth tail was scared.

The other officer walked up to my car, and when I saw it was the sergeant, I got a big Kool-Aid smile on my face. This Sergeant was a fan of mine. He was an older officer who always liked giving advice and loved talking to me, just because.

The sergeant was also his supervisor, and you couldn't arrest anyone without approval from the supervisor.

The sergeant spoke with Officer Flashlight, then came up to the window and was like, "Emori? Emori, what happened? And did you call him a flashlight cop?"

I explained my side of how I saw things and admitted that I did call him Mr. Flashlight Cop. The sergeant then told me the officer wanted to arrest me and had six tickets ready to hand me. I got quiet.

He said, "I'm going to handle these, but you have to apologize for calling that man Flashlight Cop. You do know we are certified peace officers, and you owe him that respect."

"Sorry, Sergeant."

"Go on home now, Emori, and stay out of trouble." And I did stay out of trouble, at least for the remainder of that night. But for some reason, this was my season of run-ins with law enforcement.

A week later we had a football game and we won. It was late, well into the wee hours, and a couple of my friends and I were hanging in the lounge area at the Towers—that's the dorms. Boys' rooms were on the left, and the girls' on the right. I had moved off campus by this time and was just hanging out up there. We began talking with a few of the campus police who were hanging around. One of the officers was from Chicago, and I was from Milwaukee, so we had much to talk about. In the meantime, my friends had wandered off, and so did the other officer.

As we talked, just the two of us now, I put my head down on the desk, trying to listen. But I was tired, and it was late, and I fell asleep. When I looked up and saw the sun was starting to break. I said, "Let me go home."

He nodded. "Be careful driving home because the sergeant isn't working right now to save you."

I looked at him in question, then laughed. "Well, maybe there won't be any sensitive officers out there." This began a wonderful friendship that led to him being my soul mate—Jimmy Alexander, the love of my life.

He was the male version of me, and I was the female version of him. He stood six foot two, and yes, he was bald with beautiful caramel skin. I loved everything about this man. Well, not everything.

Over time we were stuck together like glue, or at least like Velcro. He played tennis and was a math genius. He had a smart mouth as much as I gave it. He threw it. He was my match. He knew when I needed a hug versus when I needed a thug. He was the only man who could handle me.

> So, let's be realistic. Can you date you? Most of us want a man who can handle us. And when I say handle us, I mean a man who knows me enough to know when I'm fussing, am I really upset about something or is it I need some loving? If I'm complaining, is that really the problem? And if you know how to handle your woman, you'll know what words to say to put her into action or a mood.
>
> I was told if your man can't calm you down when you're upset, he can't be your

> man. That comes from a mature man pay-
> ing attention to details about the woman he
> says he wants to be with.

Jimmy knew me, and knew how to handle me. Jimmy knew how to love me. He adored me and was crazy about me, or he was before he got to know me better. It was just bad timing for us.

Jimmy had heard about the incident of the girl in the white Camry that Sergeant saved. It had spread all around the AUC police departments. I would soon become the talk of the town among police officers. For some, it was a good thing. For others, well, not so much. For Jimmy, it intrigued him. He had to find out more about the young lady who had the sergeant wrapped around her fingers.

Jimmy would work the morning watch and most days when he got off, he would come to my place until I left for class. We developed a relationship away from the school, and when we were at the school, we pretended like nothing was going on between us. Now for me, it was easy. For Jimmy, yeah, not so much.

I was popular around school, into a lot of organizations and volunteering. I encouraged kids to come to my school. My school was my life, and I was passionate about my life. Plus, I had older cousins there, and my big brother went there. I had a legacy. Topping all that I was an all-around nice person. I was gifted at helping other kids not feel so homesick. At one time, I had a whole planned-parenthood connection for all types of birth control. I was the campus plug for birth control.

Jimmy had a way of making me feel important. He spoiled me. He would wash my car, and he knew I wouldn't go get gas at night, so he would always meet me to pour my gas or at least sit in the squad car and watch me.

I remember calling him to say, "Hey, I'm ready to leave campus now, but I don't have enough gas to get home."

He would simply say, "Go ahead, I'll meet you there."

He was my dream guy. But I was too young to recognize that this was the kind of man a girl should marry. I was stuck on if the sex ain't great, we weren't great.

I knew nothing about juvenile diabetes, which is what he had. I just knew having sex with him was too much of a chore, and I didn't like it. Now, keep in mind, I was a young college student. I had guys for days after me, and let's just say I wasn't turning down much of nothing but my collar. Jimmy had everything but sex; his soldier boy wouldn't rise to the occasion. I didn't know it was medical until I got older.

The semester would soon come to an end. This would be my first semester staying over the summer. I had my car and a part-time job, and I thought I could handle not going home. But the bills started piling up, and I couldn't maintain an apartment on a part-time salary. Plus, I wanted to go home. I had gotten homesick and was not ready to be a full-grown adult.

I went to Jimmy and said, "There are six weeks left for the summer. I think I'm going home until school starts."

"You've already made your decision, and you're just leaving?"

"Yes, I'm leaving. But I'll be back in a few weeks." I left, not knowing what damage I was doing to him or our relationship. Well, I was young and just having fun, or so I thought.

It was now a week before I was to return to Atlanta. Jimmy and I had talked off and on over the summer but nothing too serious. I called him and said, "Hey, I'll be back this Friday."

He said, "Okay," and sounded really nonchalant about me returning.

I expected him to be excited. He was going to get to see me again. But something sounded off. I asked him, "Is there anything you want to tell me before I come back?"

"No."

"Well, okay. Is there anything you *need* to tell me before I get back? There's a difference between you wanting to tell me something and you needing to tell me before I find out. If so, tell me now."

"There's nothing to tell."

"Okay, cool." And I'd asked him this question over the phone specifically because I knew I would have a twelve-hour drive to get over it.

He didn't ask me the same questions, so I didn't have to lie or tell him about my summer with Iggy and Sam and how I got busted with those two. Yeah, that's another story for another time. But the point was, there was nothing to tell because he said there was nothing to tell. So, I took his word.

I got back and set up another new apartment in Stone Mountain. I got another job doing customer service, plus I was back in school. Jimmy and I picked right back up where we left off without missing a beat.

A month went by, and I was studying to become a member of the Order of Eastern Star. Jimmy was a Mason. I finished up and added Eastern Star to my list of accomplishments. I crossed and so now I needed to study to know my craft. I studied with one of the brothers, who was at the ceremony for Eastern Star, and who had attended Morris Brown College previously. He knew my oldest brother and was once friends with him.

After I crossed, this guy said, "Come with me." We went back to his place, and I thought nothing of it. I thought of him as my big brother. Apparently, he didn't think of me as his little sister. He bragged around campus that he had taught this sister in one night her stuff. "She's a bad mama jamma. She learned everything in a matter of hours, and I taught it to her. Oh, she ready, she ready." But in his telling of the story to a bunch of guys in the police station, he made it sound intimate and sexual, and he was bragging, not realizing Jimmy was my man and had no clue about this little study session.

I pulled up to the station just to say hi to my man, and I walked into an ambush.

One of the officers pulled me in and said, "So I hear you know your stuff." I, Ms. Overly Confident, Ms. Too-Smart-for-Your-Own-Good, took the challenge and didn't back down. It was Jimmy and three other Masons who were police officers and one sister KK. They made KK not say a word and told her she couldn't help me.

They threw question after question at me, and I was eating those questions up. I was killing it, doing too well for my own good. Then my man, the man I slept with at night, the man I once cooked dinner for, asked a simple question, and I couldn't answer it.

They were like, "Whoa. How did you miss that one?" Those men were so impressed by my knowledge and how fast I had learned. But Jimmy was pissed.

He said, "Go, get outta here until you learn the basics."

Everyone laughed but was like, "Nah, Jimmy, she's still tight. She learned quite a bit in a short time."

We got outside, and everyone else had gone their way. Jimmy was fuming hot. "What the hell were you doing in this man's bedroom? Why were you at his house?"

"He asked me to. He wanted to go change clothes, and we were just studying. It wasn't a big deal."

"Yes, it was! This man has gone around telling everyone how he taught you from his bedroom."

"Whoa. He's making it sound like he and I had done something. That's not the case."

"Hell, I know. But everyone else may not."

"Look, I'll talk to him."

"No, you won't. Not ever again. And you better not ever go back to his place."

The next day, I learned the two of them had an exchange of words that were not good. I smoothed things over with Jimmy, and we were cool.

A few weeks later, KK and I were sitting in the booth just talking. And remember, no one knew about Jimmy and me. KK was giving me the campus gossip from over the summer—the six weeks I was gone.

She began to tell me about Jimmy and a certain dorm assistant. About how they were flirting back and forth and then went out to dinner at Benihana. I was very interested in this story, about how it started and what happened, and how it ended or was it still going. She told me she heard the date went well, but out of the blue, he just stopped talking to her and didn't go anywhere past that one date.

"Oh really?" Now my questions started. "When did he all of a sudden just stop talking to her?"

"I'm not sure, but I think around the time school started back."

I couldn't wait until she and I were done talking. I practically flew to where he was. I needed answers. I called him, and I asked, "Where are you?"

"I'm by my house, heading to Walmart."

"Fine, I'll meet you there."

I pulled up and was like, "I asked you if there was anything you wanted to tell me before I came back here. I knew whatever it was, I could handle it because I would have the twelve-hour drive to get over it. But you chose not to tell me about you and Ms. Dorm Assistant."

He shrugged. "It was nothing. Just a little dinner."

"But you didn't tell me."

"You left me. Right in the middle of us, you left me."

"I came back, and I was only gone for a few weeks. It was no big deal."

"It was a big deal. You didn't say you needed anything. You just left me."

That's when I knew I had brought up old pain for him. He said I abandoned him when I left. I wasn't paying attention because I had too many men in the fire to pay attention to just one. I had caused him more pain.

We left there, and I was feeling bad. I realized then that my homesickness had caused him pain. We fell off after that. We weren't as close. We started pulling apart but not far apart.

I remember one night at the school, after a game, just hanging out in the lounge of the dorms, a few police officers and me and my girls. We all were standing there, laughing and talking. One of the officers made a pass at me in front of everyone. Yep, everyone, including Jimmy. By now, one of Jimmy's police officer friends knew about him and me, and my girls Kasia and Kim knew. I think this officer suspected something but either wasn't sure or didn't care because he made a pass at me anyway.

I was a big flirt. I talked a big game, but I wasn't going to do anything. Then when he made the pass at me, I was thrown way off guard. Maybe because Jimmy was standing there, and I didn't know how to play that one off, so I didn't. I flirted back with the guy. Jimmy's standing there, laughing and shaking his head and shaking his foot too, and I wasn't catching none of the clues Jimmy was sending off. But my girl Kim was.

She was like, "Okay, well then, we're going to go. Emori, come drop us off at our dorm. Now!" I agreed, and we left.

The next day, in the same dorm, we're all together again, hanging in the lounge. But this time, a student guy was flirting with me, and I was flirting back. Hey, it's flirting. It's meaningless, right? Wrong. It's misleading.

But now, a female student was flirting with Jimmy. I petted the game. I went over, interrupted their conversation and pulled him outside. I was like, "What the hell was that?" and I hit the tip of his hat, sending it off his head.

He snatched his hat and was like, "Go now, E. You're sitting there constantly flirting in my face, and when somebody says something to me, now you're jealous?"

Yup, we had a little disagreement that led to me to leaving with a guy friend of mine. Needless to say, Jimmy was pissed.

Well, I was dog-sitting, and I needed someone to go with me to check on the dogs. And James was available. James also had feelings for me, but I didn't know. Well, that was until he expressed them to me that night.

I had to let James know I was involved with Jimmy, and I didn't feel the same way that he did. But this was the beginning of the end of Jimmy and me.

I remember one time the sergeant sent for me. Now when the sergeant sends for you, you had better go.

I went to his office, and he was like, "Emori, you're a good kid with a bright future ahead of you. I don't want to see you mess that up."

"Well, thank you, sir."

"You know Officer Alexander, don't you?"

"Yes, I do, sir."

"Well, is there anything going on with you two?"

"Excuse me, sir?"

"Do you two have a personal relationship?"

"No, sir. But his brother and I do."

"Oh, okay. I am glad to hear that."

I left out of there, and I went to class, laughing and thinking, *whew*. I just got called into the principal's office.

Now I hadn't seen or talked to Jimmy all that day. Later, after school, Jimmy came over, and he said, "Hey, I got called into sergeant's office today about you."

I looked at him and at the same time said, "I got called into the sergeant's office about you."

We laughed, and he asked, "Well, what did you tell him?"

"I said that I was seeing your brother."

Jimmy fell out laughing. "That's the same thing I told him." We laughed so hard together about how we could, without a heads-up or a warning, give the exact same lie and not even know it. That was how in tune with each other we were.

But still, we broke up, and for the life of me, I cannot give you the exact reason for our break-up. All I know is we never got over each other.

> How many of y'all know that men are just as messy as women? They talk and talk and gossip too.

The following semester would come, and a new officer would catch my attention. For some reason, I had a thing for men in uniform. This guy was six foot five, chocolate dark, and too handsome for my own good. And yes, he too was bald. We would flirt out loud and in public. He was younger than Jimmy, a little closer in age to me and didn't know much about discretion; he was out in the open telling folks he gon' make me his gal. Yes, he was a country boy too. In his mind, I was above legal age, so he didn't care that I was a student and he worked there.

After a season of flirting back and forth and sexually trash talking, we made plans to go out. Once I knew he was serious about going out, I said, "You need to know something, and it's best if I tell you now before someone else does."

He's looking all nervous. "Okay, what's up?"

"Well, you should know I've dated someone you work with."

"Oh yeah?"

"Now, before you ask me, I'm not telling you who it was. I'm simply making you aware of why I want to keep this thing between us quiet and low-key."

"Okay, no problem."

We proceeded to finish making our date plans, but the next day, Mr. Lover Boy was quiet as a church mouse. He didn't have many conversations with me. When he saw me in passing, he barely spoke.

I'm thinking, wait a minute, what's up with this? So, I caught him later and asked him just that. "What's up? You seem different and quiet."

"I got a lot on my mind. So, you used to date Officer Alexander, huh?"

I put my hands over my face and shook my head. "Didn't I tell you not to ask who?" Now I wanted him not to ask for two reasons. One, I knew Jimmy was his supervisor. And two, I knew men were messy, and Jimmy and his crew wouldn't let that man be.

I said to him, "Is that going to be a problem for you?"

"No. No, it won't be for me," and I left there, thinking, yep, this one's over. It wasn't over because he knew; it was over because I knew better.

The next day I ran into one of Jimmy's guys, Pat. We said hi in passing, then I made a U-turn and asked, "Which one of you told him, and what did you say to him?"

He knew exactly what I was talking about. He was laughing and asked, "Well, what did you think was going to happen? The dude asked, and someone told him it was Jimmy. And then the fool went to Jimmy and asked Jimmy if it was true. Jimmy told the man, 'You can date her. But she'll always be mine, and it definitely won't last long because I ain't going nowhere.'"

Yup, that date didn't happen, and Mr. Lover Boy abruptly stopped talking to me altogether. Of course, I was in my feelings a little bit with oh, now he's cock-blocking me.

Still, even with all this drama, Jimmy and I remained friends—close friends—until he died.

Oh, I have to remind myself to come back to this later in the story. I have to tell you what happened when I found out about Jimmy's death. But before I do, I have to introduce the other person in that story, so keep reading. It gets greater later.

I'll forever love me some Jimmy Alexander.

CHAPTER 4

Hypothetically Speaking

Hypotheticals are possible situations, statements or questions about something imaginary rather than something real. According to *Webster's Dictionary*, it is a noun—a hypothetical proposition or statement. Hypotheticals deal with the concept of what-if.

Per *Wikipedia*, a one-night stand is a single sexual encounter in which there is an expectation that there shall be no further relations between the sexual participants.

Okay, so, are we good? We just learned the formal meaning of a few words I want you to keep in mind because, in this next story, you'll need to know those legal terms to understand what really occurred.

Life consists of many little moments compounding into one big ole bowl called life decisions. And did you know you're free to choose but not free from the consequences?

A one-night stand means you'll never see or speak to them again. So, if you made the decision to enjoy a one-night stand, hopefully, you were smart enough to use a condom and not have to deal with the consequences of having to see that person again. Unfortunately, many don't; hence, the success of shows the likes of Maury and Jerry.

> I have always been free in my sexuality. However, safety was always a priority. I would teach sex education and sexual acts to other women. Yeah, I learned a little early

that it's more than what you can do in the kitchen that holds a man's attention.

One night, when I was an RA (resident assistant) in college, I was in my room doing nothing, and one of my floormates, Quetta, came to my door and asked for a goodie bag. In these goodie bags, as I called them, were lubricants, condoms, female condoms, and birth control pills. Anything to prevent pregnancy, I had it. Yes, you'll recall me saying earlier that I and planned parenthood had a thang going on. I knew where the abortion clinics were and the rules to get in the door. I knew the rules and policies on when you could have one and when you shouldn't. I was the go-to girl.

Quetta asked me what I was up to, and I told her nothing.

"But it's Friday night. Come out with me. Come get out. Besides, my guy has a roommate who's just returning from boot camp."

I thought about it and was like, "Okay, cool, let's go." I got cute and went on with her. Not only did she need the goodie bag, but she had got me to tag along with her as the wingman. I didn't realize when I got there it would be this fine bald chocolate man that I would meet.

I had a thing about men being older and taller than me. In my mind, they both provided security. If he was tall, he could cover me and protect me; and if he was older, he was done with the games and had more stability.

Now, these things were part of my checklist. I had no clue they were all fantasy-island-type reasons.

That night we played games and drank, and I really enjoyed hanging out. Later, the only couple there soon retired off into their private room of the apartment. Me and Mr. One Time continued to talk and laugh, watch TV and drink a little more.

Well, time moved on into the morning hours, and now things seemed to progress with us fairly well, so much so that I ended up in Mr. One Time's bedroom showing him my massaging skills.

I worked with the school's football team as a trainer, and I'd told him how I helped the football guys recover with therapy in my college work-study program. And he was explaining to me how he had been injured at boot camp.

Okay, it was probably a plow to get me to touch him in private. Well, I fell for it, and boy, oh boy, did I get to touch him. Then he got to touch me, and some things started happening with some kissing below the belt, and then some clothes came off, and it was on and popping. I couldn't stop this train from leaving the station if I wanted to. And I was pretty sure I didn't want to.

The next day the sun came up, and us girls left. I never went back. Quetta and I never talked about that night again.

Spring came, and one day I was walking down the street headed into the SAQ dormitory on my college campus. I saw my boo Jimmy standing there, talking to a group of other guys. Now keep in mind our relationship was a secret. Therefore, he couldn't react much when he saw things happening that he didn't like with me.

As I walked toward this group of men—well, this group of police officers—they were blocking the stairways that led to where I was headed, so I spoke to everyone in general. "Hello, everyone. Excuse me."

They spoke and shifted. Then, of course, Jimmy had to say something extra. "Your classes aren't this way." All the guys turned and looked at me and kind of laughed.

I responded with, "Neither is my daddy standing that way."

The others, of course, said "Ohhh" and laughed.

I turned back and started walking away until this guy who stood in the middle of the group stopped me. "Don't I know you?"

I looked at him, and everyone stopped talking and looked at me. "Excuse me?"

This time he said, "Yeah, I do know you."

"I'm sure you have me mixed up with someone else. But nice to meet you."

One of the other officers said, "Emori, this is Officer One Time."

I came back to shake his hand, looked him in his eyes, and said to him, "That's a nice pickup line, but it doesn't work on me." I fluttered my lashes and turned to walk away.

He said, "Your roommate is Quetta."

I stopped and slowly turned around. "Who are you again?"

He smiled—well, laughed, really—and started toward me while all the other officers moved clear out of the way. Of course, Jimmy stood there, looking all curious.

Now, most of the officers either knew about Jimmy and me or assumed there was something between him and me. So, for another officer to call your girl out as this guy did, the way he did, caused some eyebrows to raise.

So, he stands right in front of me, and I'm thinking long and hard, *Do I know this man? Oh, Lawd, what have I forgotten?*

"I'm Mr. One Time. You and Quetta came over to me and my roommate's place earlier this year."

So, in my mind, that was last semester. And yes, I totally forgot about him. I smiled and said, "It was nice meeting you."

Mr. One Time was holding my hand by this time, and we were both smiling. Jimmy walked over and said, "So you do know him."

"I believe so," I replied while looking at Mr. One Time. "If I remember, you were not an officer."

"I wasn't then, but I would love to talk to you about it."

> Ladies, why do we get caught up and in love so quickly that we forget the art of dating? If he hasn't placed a ring on your finger, he is your friend. Therefore, you should continue to date.
>
> No one is saying to have sex with every guy you meet. No, but considering all options is a must. We are so in love while they are sowing their royal oats with Susie Mae and every Rae they pass. But keep it classy, ladies, not trashy.

I said, "I have an appointment right now, but it was nice meeting you."

He said, "Oh, you've met me."

I chuckled. "Right," I replied while holding my finger up. "Hopefully, I'll see you again." And I walked off.

Behind me, I heard the guys all laughing as they started walking off. Well, Jimmy didn't find anything about it funny.

Before I got all the way into the building, I turned around, and at the same time, Mr. One Time turned around as well. I waved for him to come back, and he did.

I asked him for his number, and he gave me his business card. "Uhm, maybe I'll call you, or maybe I won't."

"You better."

Now I had to keep my cool in front of my ex-boyfriend at the time, Jimmy. I couldn't let him see me sweat.

One-night stands are supposed to be just that—a one-time occurrence, never to see that person again. So, how is it months later he impressed me by remembering me when I had totally put him and that night out of my mind?

Now I'm still me, and it's hard to capture my attention. It took me a month or so to actually call him, but I did, and we immediately hit it off. The conversations were intriguing, and we had so much to talk about.

We met up not long after that, and no, it wasn't for sex or about sex. By this time, I was working at a group home, and he came over to my apartment, which was a building where teens and young women lived in their individual places.

Anyway, he would come over, and we would laugh and talk and share goals. We started to see each other regularly and talk more often. I remember him applying for a police officer's job at Marta. We worked on his resume and prayed about his interview; it was exciting, especially once he actually got the job. He became a smart officer. His shifts were at first irregular, and I would see him less often then, but we would still talk.

My brother had died before this time, and I had never really mourned his death. But one night after talking with Mr. One Time, my brother came to me in a dream, and it really scared me. I was young and had never experienced death so close to me before.

I woke up and called Mr. One Time in the early morning, and he came over immediately. He held me and comforted me until I was no longer scared.

I made love to Mr. One Time that morning, and it really felt different. I cried while we were having sex. It wasn't normal sex. It wasn't the "Wham, bam, thank you, ma'am kind." This was sensual and sexual and intimate—very intimate. I had never experienced anything like it before. And since our actual "one-night stand," this was the first time we'd had sex. It wasn't planned; it wasn't plotted. It was just so intimate and loving and caring, and it caused me to look at him differently. I mean, I really looked at him.

The days went on, and he and I became closer and closer. Then, one day when he was coming over, I decided I had to show him I could burn in the kitchen as well as in the bedroom. I cooked him my famous steak and twice-baked potatoes and green beans for dinner—every ghetto girl's starter dinner set. I had his favorite bottle of liquor and lots of candles lit, just waiting for his arrival. I was dressed all so pretty and ready and waiting. He never showed; he got called into work.

I was sad and disappointed. So much so that I went to his job to take the meal I had specially prepared just for him.

Nope, I didn't tell him I was coming. Okay, it was a trust thing. I didn't believe him, and if I told him I was coming, he would make an excuse, or so I thought. But he was really there.

He was really at work. I hugged him, left the food, and went home with a smile. Later, he called to thank me.

I'm not sure when or how, but things began to shift between Mr. One Time and me after that. I really started feeling something for him.

A few weeks went by, and Mr. One Time showed up at my place. I was so excited to see him that I didn't complain about him popping up unannounced. Now, normally it would have been a whole production. After all, I can't have men popping up at my place unexpectedly. He might run into the next guy. Everyone had a schedule, so they didn't run into each other.

So, while we were standing outside, he said, "Let me ask you a hypothetical question."

"Sure, what's up?" I replied as I was holding his neck.

"Hypothetically, what would you do if I said a girl I knew was pregnant? What would you say?"

"Oh, I would be cool. No big deal." And I shrugged.

"No big deal? That's what you would say?"

I said yes and started talking about something else. I didn't take the time to really listen to what he *wasn't* saying. I only heard what he said and brushed it off. It really was no big deal to me.

But outta nowhere, he slowly started ghosting me—not returning my calls, not coming over as much—until one day he was just gone. And I have always been that chick. The "I ain't chasing no man, there are too many out there" chick. But I was quite curious as to why he ghosted me? Things had been taking off so well. We were connecting on different levels. He was a go-getter, a motivator, and we made each other better.

After two weeks of no calls, no show, I popped up at his job. What did I do that for? Well, let me tell you, this was where life took me into a swirl pool. Out of nowhere, my core was shaken.

So, my cousin Lynn and I went to see a show at Uptown Comedy in Buckhead. Laughter really does the heart good. But it didn't take Mr. One Time off my heart.

On the way there, I explained to Lynn the situation. "This guy just ghosted me with no trail of crumbs as to why." Lynn was gracious or maybe just nosey, but after the show, she drove me to his job, which was up the street from there in Lindberg. When I got there, I asked another officer to go get Mr. One Time. After a fifteen to twenty-minute wait, he finally came out. I looked at him, and he looked at me with a smile on his face.

I said, "What's up?"

"What's up with you?"

"So, we're not into returning calls."

"I've been busy."

> I learned a long time ago that you make time for what's important to you. If I was important enough to him, he would have found time. This should have been a clue to my blind self. But nope, I had to push the envelope. I wanted answers. It was messing with my self-esteem. I leave guys; they don't leave me. But he ghosted me and didn't look back for me.

I said, "So what's really going on because something doesn't smell quite right."

Mr. One Time looked at me and said, "Wow, you look absolutely gorgeous."

"Focus, Mr. One Time, focus! We were hitting it off so well. I thought we were headed for the next level. What the hell happened? And I want the truth."

He looked at me in disbelief. "I told you."

"Quit playing. We haven't talked."

"The girl was pregnant, and I married her."

"What?" Then I put my head down, took a deep breath, and said, "Bet."

He had a look of surprise and asked why I was upset.

"Dude, you just said you married someone and got a baby on the way. That cancels me out altogether."

"But you said it was no big deal."

"You said that was a hypothetical question, not real life, not *your* real-life situation."

"I thought you knew."

"How was I supposed to know? You haven't talked to me in almost a month."

I turned to get back in the car with my cousin, and she could see it on my face. "Hey, hey, keep it together until we pull off. Hold on, one second."

And she was right. I held my head up and didn't shed a tear. I held on tight—well, that was until we got on the highway. I then shed a tear, alright.

Wow, the pregnant ex got the ring.

What was the lesson in this? I had started falling for a guy, and it wasn't about sex. How we met turned into something out of the ordinary. We developed a friendship that became deep and was important to both of us.

Later, I would cry, but once I got over the initial shock of him marrying a woman just because she was carrying his child, I realized his decision had nothing to do with me. It had nothing to do with if I was good enough, and it had nothing to do with if I was smart enough. It had nothing to do with me at all and everything to do with him and his soon-to-be child. He chose his future legacy over a newly founded friendship. He didn't break any promise to me. We were dating, not obligated. This was a painful lesson to learn, but a lesson learned nonetheless.

A year went by before I could ever speak to him again. I would sometimes see him on a Marta train while riding to my new job. He wouldn't see me. Then one day, he was with a group of officers and called my name really loud. He then came over and hugged me tight. It was in this embrace that I would realize I'd forgiven him. It was in this embrace that I would start a true friendship, not a friendship that would ever lead to love or marriage but the love of a friend, a confidant, one where we would be able to confide in each other—a dependable friend.

He left his coworkers that day and completed my ride with me. We caught up with each other. He had a beautiful little girl. He had married his little girl's mother. He wouldn't speak of his wife much but a whole lot about his baby girl. He asked if we could be friends again.

"Let me think about it," I said as I exited the train."

Hypothetically Speaking

"Call me, girl. I miss you." I waved goodbye as the train doors closed with a sense of peace about him and about that situation. I no longer felt sliced or like I had gotten the short end of the stick. I was at peace knowing he truly married her because she was pregnant and didn't want his child to grow up without a father as he did. Who could be upset with a man for being a man and owning his responsibility? Yes, he liked his wife, and I'm sure he grew to love her eventually. But either way, I was fine with me.

Eventually, I called him, and every so often, we would see each other as friends. We would hang out and talk about goals and dreams of what we wanted outta this life. He said I motivated him. I just held him accountable for what he said he wanted.

I watched him grow from a horny little boy into an amazing man. Mr. One Time and I became good friends. I knew he was married while I was single, and we had slept together more than once. And I knew if we were going to really be friends, I had to meet his wife.

Each time we saw each other, whether it was an accidental meeting or intentional, I made sure to always bring his wife up and ask about her. I would tell him, "Hey, I want to meet your wife." He would always say okay and quickly move on to speaking about something else. It never really dawned on me that he was purposeful in not allowing me to meet her. I couldn't pick this lady out in a lineup. I had no clue what she looked like or even her name, for that matter. I knew everything about her daughter and husband and nothing about her.

Years later, I ran into his best friend, Bam, and we talked. I mentioned to Bam that I continued to ask about Mr. One Time's wife and kept asking to meet her, but it seemed like Mr. One Time planned to ignore me.

Bam laughed. "Yes, he is ignoring you."

I asked why as I was laughing too.

"His wife knows about you. He tells her sometimes that he saw you or little things about you. But you two will never meet."

"Why? Why can't I meet her?"

Bam looked me in the eyes. "If the two of you ever met, he would be divorced soon after."

I was shocked and confused. "I don't understand."

Bam explained that Mr. One Time's wife was insecure about her marriage, her plus size, education level—just all the way insecure. She knew he only married her because she was pregnant.

"She also knew you were the woman he would have married had he not married her. You, too, are plus-size, but you're confident, a go-getter, and about your business and secure in who you are. She's not. And she knows you have the one thing she doesn't."

"Wow, really? What's that one thing?"

"His respect." And Bam walked off.

I was left with my mouth hanging open. For the first time in my life, I was speechless.

Mr. One Time and I are still friends today. I cherish the man that he is and love him all the same. To this day, some twenty years later, I have never met his wife. I have seen and met his daughters but never the wife. He remains married and is still an officer and a gentleman.

CHAPTER 5

The Bus Ride

I was young, fresh outta college, and had bright eyes and a bushy tail. I was off to my first real job after college. The new job was in a heavily trafficked area, so I took public transportation. I rode the train to the bus and the bus to my job.

Well, on my first day, I left hours early to be on time. It was my first day; I was excited. It was with a big firm. I was proud of myself for landing such a prestigious position. I wanted to make a good first-day impression. Who would have known I would meet the man of my dreams on this day?

I called the recorded line, and it told me which bus to take that would put me off right across the street from my new office. I took bus 92. I remember because '92 was the year I graduated from high school. Yes, I'm a numbers girl. Numbers mean something to me—the correlation of numbers.

So, I got on the bus and saw a friend of mine, Anita, who I hadn't seen in a while. She waved me down, and I sat next to her. We laughed and talked the whole ride together. Now keep in mind I was a nervous wreck but still excited at the same time; therefore, I was not on my p's and q's. And I was not paying full attention to my surroundings. Thank God Anita was.

She was like, "Hey, he keeps looking at you."

"Who keeps looking at me?"

"The bus driver."

I then looked toward the front of the bus and saw him adjusting his mirror. It's like the mirror was more focused in my direction.

Anita recognized it as well. "Uhm, he focused all right. He's focused on some Emori."

"He better focus on the road." I saw he was chocolate and tall and, you guessed it, bald.

Ignoring him, I kept talking to Anita while she focused on him looking at me. She was like, "Do you know him?"

"Nope, don't think so, and probably not because I'm a long way from home." As Anita was getting off the bus at her stop, she turned to me and said, "Well, he's trying to get to know you."

Now I was still on the bus and didn't realize no one else was except me and Mr. Bus Driver. Not really knowing where I was—remember I was a long way from home—yes, Dorothy, you're not in Kansas anymore—I was surprised when the bus then turned into the bus bank, and the bus driver was now parking.

He turned in his seat and said, "Ma'am, are you lost?"

"I guess so. You've just parked the bus."

"Well, it's my break and the end of the route. So, I take my break here and then go back toward the train station."

I looked around, confused and checked my watch. "Oh dear, I cannot be late on my first day." Yup, you guessed it, I was starting to panic—a full-blown panic attack.

This slick dude got up and walked toward me. "Where are you trying to go? Let me help you."

Now, what went through my mind at that moment was, *Oh my, where am I?* But then I see this tall—very tall—dark-skinned, thick like I like them, bald, very handsome man. Yes, drawls were getting wet just looking at him.

Stop it. Don't act like I'm the only woman who's ever looked at a man and started drooling/wondering what he's working with.

Well, I told him where I was trying to go. He said, "You should have taken bus 29. This is 92."

Oh, how didn't I remember 29? That's my birthdate. But nope, I got on 92, my graduation year. Yes, remember I told y'all I'm a numbers person.

"Oh, my apologies."

"None needed. Maybe we were supposed to meet." I was blushing. Yes, I, a dark-skinned gal from the valley, was blushing over this large chocolate country-talking boy. He said, "Let me go back early, so you're not late for your first day."

I was thinking, *Hmmm, that's a sacrifice. That's him paying attention to my needs.*

Wait! I was not falling in love at first sight. Okay, maybe I was. This man appeared to have all the pieces to make the perfect chocolate cake.

He pulled back out and began to drive, and we began talking. He told me he had one daughter, not married. I told him this was my first job after college. I had no kids. He was from the Dirty South; I was from the Midwest. Yes, this was how long the ride was. It was like talking to a long-lost friend. He was easy to talk to and held my attention. He calmed me down and kept me from panicking about being late.

We got back to the train station, and he was like, "Your chariot awaits. Bus 29." I hurried off so as not to miss my bus. I was mesmerized by this man. Yup, I quickly snapped back to reality.

I could not be late for my first day. I ran off the bus, caught the correct one, and we were on our way. I had made the bus by my skinny chin-chin.

I made it to my first day of work just in time. I wasn't late, but I wasn't early like I had planned and wanted to be.

I was sitting there in orientation, thanking God for his grace and mercy for allowing me to make it in time. After orientation class begun, I started drifting off thinking about how my morning went, and then it hit me. Yup, you guessed it. I did not get his number, nor did I give him mine. I was in complete devastation. Like how did I let that happen?

Well, now I was at my new job, deep in my feelings, daydreaming about a man I would never see again, and boy, oh boy, was he something to daydream about, He fit my idea of a perfect man, so how did I let that slip through my hands? He embodied what a man should be—well, in my mind. He was the perfect specimen, and I didn't get his number.

Now I couldn't focus. I couldn't concentrate. I couldn't believe I'd let this happen to me, Ms. Flirt. No, not me! But yeah, I let it happen. What can I say? It was what it was, and I just had to live with the fact that I let a specimen like that slip through my hands.

I soon got over it and completed my workday. I rode bus 29 back to the train station with no more thoughts of Mr. Bus Driver. I couldn't let it ruin my day. It had occupied my mind for the entire morning. I made it home and continued my life as it was. I enjoyed my new job and meeting new people.

The next morning, it was time to do it all over again. I got dressed, got in my car, drove to the train station, got on the train, and then went to the next train station where I would catch bus 29. Well, guess which bus was sitting there when I got there? Yup, you got it, bus 92.

I walked up the steps to the bus loop, and the first thing I saw was this tall, dark, handsome bald man in navy-blue pants and a light-blue uniform shirt with his shiny black shoes. He was just standing there, awaiting my arrival, or so I wanted to believe.

In my mind, no one else existed at that moment but the two of us. He was standing outside his bus, eating an apple and waiting on me—well, waiting on passengers to board the bus. I was looking at the schedule to see what time bus 29 came.

He politely said, "Excuse me, ma'am, are you lost again?"

I slowly looked up, and we both started laughing. "No, sir. I'm actually looking for the time when my correct bus comes since you don't wanna go my way."

"I'll gladly take you anywhere you want to go, Ms. Lady."

I smiled so big, probably too big. I was thinking this is where he saw the she's-a-fool sign on my face. "Well, I would need your seven digits to make that happen."

He quickly sang that number to me, and I had to move fast to write it down. As he turned to throw the apple away, he said, "I hope you don't forget it," then boarded his bus and pulled off. I was scrambling, looking for a pen in my purse to write it down. Now you best be believing I did not forget that number.

It turned out to be his pager number. Yes, this is a '90s story, and I said beeper, pager, old-school communication device.

I went to work just as happy as a Bessie bug. I got home and couldn't wait to text him. He called back within minutes, and the talking continued all week long.

Then Friday appeared, and we made plans. I invited him over the next day. He accepted!

When he arrived, he looked as good as ever—freshly shaved head just shining, chocolate skin just as smooth as a baby's bottom. I was mesmerized by his beauty. He walked in with that Denzel swag. I screamed loudly in my head as he passed. My soul was like *Yesss Gawd!* I offered him something to drink.

"What do you have?"

"Water and cold water." We laughed, and I asked my questions again. This time I changed the wording just to make sure I didn't miss anything. What did I ask? Basic questions like, "Why do you just have one daughter, and how long have you been working for Marta? Where are you from?"

He began by telling me he was from Bankhead. Now we're talking about Bankhead and the historical value that is missing being said about that area. He's talking passionately about his family and his upbringing, and I was listening intensely. He held my undivided attention. I was actually intrigued. For me, that was a huge deal.

I was a person who didn't value men. I was not easily swayed by a man or anything that he had to say. Well, I was a young woman who had daddy issues, don't forget. But this man held my attention, and I was enjoying every minute of it.

I asked another critical question. "So how is it you're this nice guy, fine as all get out, and not married?"

That was my way of confirming that he was not married and didn't have a girlfriend, which is what he stated during our first meeting.

But, ladies, keep in mind I asked him if he was married and if he had a girlfriend. I thought that was all I needed to ask. Well, apparently not!

I met Mr. Bus Driver on Tuesday, July 20. He came over that Friday, and we talked daily from there. This man would soon become the man I enjoyed spending time with. From work to school and everything in between, this man got all of my free time. We would spend days and nights together. He didn't technically spend the night, but he was with me in the night, sometimes leaving at two or three in the morning. He worked split shift schedules with Marta. Meaning he would have to be at work from 6:00 a.m. until 10:00 a.m. and then again from 2:00 p.m. until 6:00 p.m., so peak hours.

Over time he stopped asking if he could stop by and would just appear. It never dawned on me that this was an act of control, where he just popped up at my place. I was sure he did it when I wasn't home a time or two but never mentioned it to me.

Mr. Bus Driver and I had been going at it pretty heavy for months, and the holidays were coming up. And holiday time to me meant family time. I couldn't take off work. I had planned to stay in the A and house-hop by my friends' parents' places and enjoy some turkey. I had Benita's house, Tasha's parents' place, and yup, the desert by KK's house. She made the best peach cobbler I had ever tasted besides my momma's. So, I was straight for the holidays.

Sista E

Mr. Bus Driver asked me what my plans were. "Well, Thanksgiving is with friends, and for Christmas, I'm going home to Milwaukee."

"Oh yeah? So does that mean I won't see you for the holidays?"

Now in my mind, we're just kickin' it—no titles, no strings, just enjoying each other. This man became upset at my plans. "I wanted you to meet my parents."

My mouth hit the ground. Now, why would my mouth hit the ground? This man was fine and employed. Plus, he laid the pipe all the way right! Well, bedroom, bathroom, kitchen, and living room now that I'm thinking about it. The whole house! Never no complaints. He kept the motion in the potion in play constantly. You would have thought we were rabbits by the way we would get it on. He's introducing me to new positions, upgrading old positions, and we were just in positions. He knew exactly how to get me right. Lawd, the memories.

Wait, where was I in this story? Oh, right. He wanted me to meet his parents. Sorry, flashbacks got me thinking back.

Now in my mind, you only meet parents when it's a serious relationship headed toward long terms and happy forevers. Still, I stood my ground and kept my plans for the holidays, but he did start me wondering. *Is this headed somewhere? Do I love him like that? Wow, meeting the parents. Are we there already in these few short months?* Well, apparently, he was, and I didn't know it.

Now you know I am a church gal born and raised from Sunday school to worship to YPWW. Church three times on Sunday, twice on Saturday and Friday nights—yep, all church all the time. But that's another book. And as the Bible says, "Train them up, and they shall not depart." I was trained to pray. You go to the throne to get answers and directions. So, before I could take this man seriously, I needed to pray.

"Father God, I come to you a wretch and a sinner. But, God, please forgive me and guide me." Now yes, I was fornicating and sinning up a storm. But so were you. We're just talking about mine right now. But I knew my word enough to stand on his promises, and I believe the Word of God.

Mr. Bus Driver finally moved past his upset over the holidays. We were headed into spring, and he and I were still going at it. I had moved and had changed jobs by then. Remember, in December, I had prayed to God for directions on this man. "Is he really the one you have for me?"

It was now March. It was a Thursday night, and I was ready to party like it was 1999 with my girl KK. I liked older men. She liked younger men, so it worked out perfectly. It was a Thursday night—bizwiz night at JJ's. Oh, how I loved going to that hole in the wall. Y'all know the hole in the wall be having the best food and the music be poppin'. We were regulars there on Thursday nights.

Well, this breezy night in March, I was all dolled up and ready to go. KK and I got in her car, and we were getting ready to pull off, and she looked over and said, "Oh, that's a nice truck."

I said, "Sure is. It looks like it might be a nice man inside too."

"Look, it's one of yo men."

"Oh shoot, it is." It was Mr. Bus Driver. Now I hadn't heard from him much lately, but that was okay because I had others to keep me company. In fact, one or two were expecting me at JJ's this night.

I jumped out of KK's car and right into his brand-new green truck. "Hey, baby, what's up?"

He said, "Oh, I just wanted to see you. Were you heading out?"

"We sure are."

"Oh well, I'll just come with you."

Okay, y'all, my mouth hit the floor, but I had to keep a straight face.

He was like, "Is that a problem?"

"Nope, it sure isn't. Let me just tell KK." I jumped back in KK's car and was like, "Oh snap, he wants to go with us."

"Be cool. Never let him see you sweat. Keep calm!"

Understand the panic was I was going there to meet other guys whom I already had plans with. One was the DJ, and the other was Mr. Birthday Boy. He and I shared the same birthday, and yes, he was fine, bald, and rich.

KK was like, "You can do this." She was egging me on. "You can do it, E." She believed in me, and I was panicking like my life was about to end this night.

I got back into his truck and said, "Okay, let's go." The sound of the truck—whew, Lawd—would make a snowman melt in sub-zero temperatures. That's how hot that truck was. That truck and the sound it made had me falling in love with him even more.

We were on our way, and I asked him to stop at the gas station. I needed gum. No, I was trying to stall, hoping he would change his mind. "Honey, don't you have to work in the morning?"

"Yes, I do, but I can have a drink or two with you for a little bit."

Okay, so none of my tactics were working. He was still driving down MLK. We get there, and the parking lot is packed. But hey, it's JJ's. I wouldn't expect anything less. Music was jumping, and KK waited in the parking lot for us to get there. We went in, as soon as the door opened, who but who was sitting right at the door involved in a game? Yup, Mr. Birthday Boy.

He's not really paying attention, but his homeboy sure was. "Hey, KK and E." Well, KK and E had a man coming in with them. What's this about? The interest was piqued. KK was in the front. I was in the middle, and Mr. Bus Driver was behind me, holding my hand. I quickly let his hand go as I saw Mr. Birthday Boy right at the front door.

We were walking, and what happened next? The darn DJ called out my and KK's names. Why, Lawd, why? Well, I had been flirting with the DJ for weeks.

We sat down and put Mr. Bus Driver in the middle of the booth to have KK on one side and me on the other, leaving us both on the end.

We got our drinks, and Mr. Bus Driver said, "Wow, you two are pretty popular here."

KK said, "Naw, we just know a few people."

He was like, "Yeah, a lot of guys, I see."

I said, "Hey, I'm going to the bathroom right quick. I'll be right back."

Now the music was playing, folks were dancing, and it's packed in there for real. I swung by the DJ booth on my way to the bathroom, and he was like, "Where's my hug, woman?"

Sista E

    I hugged him while in the booth where no one could see me. But there was still Mr. Birthday Boy that I had to address. He was the main event for the night.

    I swung past the card table, and I spoke to everyone while standing behind Mr. Birthday Boy, all the while rubbing his back. Now, of course, Mr. Bus Driver couldn't see me rubbing, but he could see me standing there at the table.

    I was there for a brief moment because Mr. Birthday Boy was playing his card game, but there long enough for him to smile and say, "What's up, girl? I see you doing yo thang."

    I left and headed toward where his friend was who had called our names out when we walked in the door. He was KK's main event for the night. I went over and sat at his table, talking to him about KK. KK was at the table, keeping Mr. Bus Driver company. I left shortly after and brought a message back to KK from him. When I arrived at the table, these two were laughing. Mr. Bus Driver told her how he saw I was very popular. KK was like, "No, that's my guy she's over there with."

    The next thing I knew, a round of drinks were delivered to the table that we didn't order. The waitress said, "No, that gentleman ordered them for you." We laughed because it was KK's guy. And what happened next? Mr. DJ played my favorite song and shouted me out. So, I got on the dance floor, and Mr. Bus Driver followed me. Well, it's just dancing. Won't nobody really know we were together. I dance a lot anyway. I was never a drinker, but I liked going to clubs because I was a dancer and I liked to dance. We were grooving to Jiggy and having a really nice time. I was loving it because I got three dudes on the hook at one location, and none were the wiser.

The Bus Ride

We sat down after dancing, and Mr. Bus Driver said, "It's been nice, ladies. I have to go." I walked him to his car. I got all the hugs and thrills in the parking lot. And he was like, "I'll see you tomorrow to continue this."

"Sure thing, handsome."

He got into the green truck and revved that engine one time for me. He drove off, and I walked back in, smiling from ear to ear.

KK gave me a standing ovation. "I've never seen a person so cool under this much pressure before, but you are pulling it off."

No sooner than I got back in the door, here came Mr. Birthday Boy wanting to slow dance and hug and feel all over me. Well, it's crowded, so Mr. DJ couldn't see a thing. An unplanned evening pulled off with me still having everything and everyone intact! I had to pat my dang on self on the back. Yeah, this was the best I had ever done.

Now we're toward the end of March. I hadn't really seen a whole lot of Mr. Bus Driver since he got this new truck, and I was okay with it because my attention wasn't solely on him. We had never really put any titles on things. And when I asked Mr. Bus Driver about adding titles, he said, "Let's just see how it goes. We don't need titles."

Ladies, you ever heard that line before?

So, he and I were going with the flow, and everything was flowing. By this time, I had started working for the bottled water company as a customer service rep. I was in training, and there were a few of us in this training class. They told us to partner up. I linked up with this lady named Lacretia. She was sweet, and we

Sista E

hit it off immediately. She shared her life stories with me, and I shared a little of mine. We became instant friends. We spent lunch time together. After work, we would be kickin' it. Days and days went by, it's now April, and it's close to Mr. Bus Driver's thirty-fifth birthday. I had been telling my new instant friend about my boo, Mr. Bus Driver. But I never mentioned him by name, never. It just never came up. And then it happened.

Girl, what happened? The shoe dropped. God answered my prayer. Now, if you know like I know, then you know God has a sense of humor, and he is always an on-time God. He will never take away your will. He gives you free will to choose. That's why he says in his Scripture to choose you this day whom you will serve. No, my prayers weren't immediately answered. I prayed for answers and directions concerning this man in December. God answered in March.

One day at work, as the day was beginning, the show hit the fan. The shoe dropped on my little fantasy when my new instant friend said, "Emori, I think I know your dude."

I laughed it off. "Yeah, I wouldn't be surprised, honey. He is popular. He's from Bankhead, he's turning thirty-five, he's a bus driver, and went to Eastlake High School. He's tall, dark, and handsome. Yeah, I am not surprised. Everyone thinks Atlanta is big, but I promise you that six degrees of separation are definitely real."

Now keep in mind I was laughing while she looked so serious. I was like, "What?"

"No, for real, Emori." She then pulled out a picture of this really big and tall chick, who's standing next to this really tall, familiar-looking man.

The Bus Ride

"Wait a minute, this looks like... Naw, couldn't be." Yup, it was Mr. Bus Driver. But here's the kicker. It's their wedding-day picture. I flipped it over, and it said the wedding date of July 31. That was eleven days *after* I met Mr. Bus Driver.

My mouth hit the floor. Tears started flowing. I had to sit down. My new instant friend was standing there, apologizing. She said, "I have been torn all week with whether to tell you or not. But I know you're a good person, and it's clear you didn't know."

I was shaking my head with my mouth hanging open. "No, I didn't."

"I know, and I'm sorry I had to be the one to tell you."

So, after I gathered myself, the questions started flowing. Now keep in mind, I hadn't seen him all week. I hadn't heard from him all week, but I wasn't worried, nor did I have any clue. But he did! Slick muthatucka.

> Yeah, don't google that. It's made up, but you get the gist.

I asked, "How do you know him?"

"The girl in the picture is his wife. His wife is my BFF!"

Y'all, I fell out. If you got BFFs as I got, we down like four flat tires, foreva. And we tell each other everythang! So, I had been talking to his wife's BFF about her BFF's husband, who was my boyfriend. Or was he? Had we said we were exclusive? Had he said, "Baby, it's you and me?"

The many thoughts began to stream in my head. A whole movie of the last nine months started playing. Is this real? How did I get played? How did I get here? How do I get up *from* here? What happens next?

My new instant friend said, "Let's go, Emori. Let's leave from here. People are starting to stare." We left and went back to her place, and the conversation began to flow like a river.

> Okay, let's pause. Let's take a moment. Go get yourself some water and some tissue because this is where it really gets juicy. I'll wait.
>
> Are you ready? Girl, close the door and make sure nobody hears you because your mouth is about to drop, and you're going to scream as I did.
>
> Okay, so my new instant friend was the wife's BFF of my bus driver boyfriend. Are you still with me?

I asked my instant friend how, what, when, and why.

She said, "Well, I went to him, and I asked him if he knew you. He looked at me and pulled me aside and said, 'What you know about that?' I said, 'Well, we work together, and she's a sweet girl. You shouldn't be doing her like that.' He said, 'Look, grown folks mind grown-folk's business.' I told him, 'You got a week to tell her, or I will.'"

Of course, he never told me. He just disappeared.

*Now, wait, pause. Ladies, some men really are slicker than a can of oil. Remember, I had asked him twice in two different ways, "Are you married? Do you have a girlfriend?" And both times, his reply was no. Well, technically, he didn't lie. And that was his MO—***main objective. He never lied, but he omitted the truth. And an omission by any other name is a lie. He didn't have a girlfriend or a wife when I met him, but** *he did have a fiancée.* *And he never mentioned her, never!*

Now here's the juice.

My new instant friend said, "Remember the guy I told you about who I was in love with, but he had slept with my friend? Well, GG is my friend, and the guy was his friend.

Wait a minute. Huh? Say what now! What kind of country backroom orgy/swingers party y'all got going on around here? "GG is your BFF, and Mr. Bus Driver's wife slept with his friend who was your boyfriend? Did I get that right?"

She nodded, and I said, "Wow! Okay, so where do I come in in all this foolery?"

She said, "I guess he just moved onto you."

But he married her eleven days after he met me. Yes, but he had found out about his wife's affair before he married her.

Now, remember, I'm a numbers girl, so my dates are explicit and accurate. Why would he keep seeing me if he had a whole wife? *Wait, when was he with his wife because he was always at my place? Hold up. Why did he want me to meet his parents?* There were just too many questions, and they kept coming, and no one could answer them but him.

I had paged him about one hundred times, but he never responded. The next day, I called his parents' house and left a message with his nephew. Yup, I had his parents' number. I knew his nephews, and they knew me, but I didn't know he was married.

I told his nephew, "Tell your uncle he better find me before I find him."

Nephew said, "Yes, ma'am, I'll tell him."

I was *hot* and *heated*. I was about to blow a gasket. Needless to say, when I went to work the next day, there he was standing outside of his truck, waiting and eating a darn apple, looking oh so ever fine—freshly shaved bald head shining—and calling my name. "Hey, baby!"

"'Hey, baby'? Those are the words you chose to say to me?"

"Well, can we talk? I can take you home."

"Sure, let's go."

We talked, and he told me, "I'm getting a divorce."

Before I knew it, I had done smacked his face. "Don't insult my intelligence."

He cried, "I'm sorry, it was a mistake. I shouldn't have married her. It was hell before, and I still went ahead and married her. I don't live there anymore. I'm trying to get out of it. She cheated with my friend, and things just got out of hand with you and me."

We talked all night and into the morning. I didn't want to go home to my place because I didn't want to fall for the okey dokey and sleep with him. So, we were in that truck all night long. Y'all, he cried and cried and talked and talked and apologized, and yup, I flopped my legs open anyway. Well, I rode the rodeo in the truck—yup, in the parking lot, in his truck. And boy, oh boy, to rub his chocolate head. Yup, I tripped and fell on his dick just like that. I had just fallen for him. I fell for the lies, games, and bull spit.

I get out of the truck and go into my place feeling like crap. Yes, he definitely gave me a few orgasms. But on my walk of shame into my place, I truly felt ashamed and dirty. Why, this was my boyfriend. But this man was a married man. The guilt of sleeping with someone's husband just took a toll on me. I had never felt this way before. I had never felt this bad before. I knew having premarital sex was a sin, but this sin was bigger than regular ole fornication. I had done hit the highest level of sin—the sin of all sins, or so I thought, but how many of you know all sin is equally bad. I had just committed adultery.

I went and got in the shower and scrubbed and scrubbed, trying to wash the sin off me, trying to wash the adultery off of me. I had done hit rock bottom in my mind. I was the worst kind of woman to knowingly slept with a married man.

Now, this was the same man I had been sleeping with for the past nine months, so why was this any different? He's still him, and I was still me. But now I knew he was married. I knew he wasn't mine. I knew he could never marry me because he'd married her.

So many things started to play out in my head, but I finally fell asleep. I got up the next morning and went to work, and I was just a wreck. I had been up most of the night crying and thinking and feeling guilty. So much so that I looked bad, eyes all swollen and red, hair in a ponytail because I couldn't even comb it. I was just messed up. And why, oh why, did the drama immediately follow?

Keep in mind I worked at a call center. I do not know how she found out, but the wife did find out about me. I don't know if he told her because my instant friend had known or if the BFF, my instant friend, had told her. But either way, I wasn't given a heads-up about the wife knowing.

The wife, GG, called the call center and left a voicemail on my work number. I didn't answer the voicemail because I was still in the queue. Apparently, this chick called and got in the queue by lying and saying she had just been talking to me as if she was a customer. Anyway, I don't know how she got my name or knew about me. All I know is the drama kept coming.

It took her two days to get through to me on my work phone. I didn't get upset. I asked for her number and promised to call her once I was on break. When I did, I went into the breakroom.

I called her back and was like, "Yes, how may I help you since you want to call up to my workplace with your drama?"

She was like, "My drama? You're the one sleeping with a married man."

I actually paused. "I apologize. However, I did not know this man was married. And I won't be seeing him again. But if you have any further questions, you're going to need to speak with the man that you married. I can't answer any questions for you. I didn't commit to you. I didn't sleep with you. He did, so please go see him and stop calling my job." I was calm and cool. I didn't get upset. I didn't raise my voice. I didn't even get angry and call her out. I remained me. I remained confident in knowing who I was and that she was hurt and upset.

This was my lunch break, and by the end of the day, please tell me why this big ole big bird-looking chick was outside my job. Now I'm 5'5", well 5'4½", and was slender at the time. I wasn't a skinny girl. I had some meat on me. But this woman had to be 6' and darn near 300 pounds. And she's standing outside my job, upset. I didn't know who she was until my instant friend told me. Now, she knew who I was and what I looked like, but I didn't have a clue about her.

> What upset me the most about this situation was the fact that he involuntarily involved me in his bull spit. He took away my right to decide if I wanted to be in some talk show drama. He put my life in danger. This woman knew who I was. She knew where I worked, but I hadn't a clue who she was or what she looked like or even her name. That brought about a new level of mad.

I walked out and headed toward my car, right past her yelling and cursing and acting a fool on this here folks' public property. I got in my car to drive off, but she blocked me, so I got out. "Look, lady, I don't want no trouble with you, and you're too big for me to fight you. I'm telling you now, I'm going to have to pick up something and bash yo head in. But I really don't want to." I was headed toward my trunk as I said it.

She saw the bat I was pulling out, and she drove off, yelling, "This ain't over!"

Women, why do we go so hard at the other woman and not him? We were two women fighting over the one man who lied. He clearly lied to both of us, but she was coming for me? Why? I really want my sisters to stop doing that. Whether you knew he was married or had not known, he knew he was married. He remembered the day he took those lovely vows. And he was certain he took those vows. The wife knew she signed up for better or worse. I was on the outside of this marriage. But we are always mad at the wrong person.

Give him that same heat, that same energy. Be mad at him; address him.

Now, women, at the same time, we have to take responsibility for our actions and stop interrupting others' marriages on purpose just because we want the dick or we don't want to be alone. Because the truth is, that's her husband, and nine times out ten, he ain't going nowhere. They will kiss and make up, and you'll still be sitting there hoping and praying he leaves her. Sis, he ain't leaving. No matter what his mouth says, what do his actions say? Can he show you a divorce decree or even an application *for divorce? A plan of action for coparenting? What can he provide to show you he is actually making steps to really get that divorce?*

Now let's say by some slim chance, he really does get a divorce. Why do you think he won't put you in the wife's position and then cheat on you? Do you really think your pussy is platinum, and it can't happen to you? Well, let me tell you. That's exactly what Mr. Bus Driver did to me.

After the wife came to my job attempting to fight me, he disappeared. I didn't call him, nor did I go looking for him. It wasn't until a month later that I heard a peep from Mr. Bus Driver.

He caught me on Memorial Day weekend, which was also his birthday weekend, by just showing up at my apartment. I didn't know if he thought he was going to get some cuttie or if he was just taking a chance and stalking me. But I looked at this fool and was like, *What could you possibly want?*

I finally opened the door. "Yes, Mr. Bus Driver, how can I help you?" He started to apologize, and I stopped him dead in his tracks. "You've already sung that song before. I know the lyrics." I stepped closer to him and lowered my voice. "Get a new tune. And for the record, I don't want to see you, smell you, and definitely don't want to hear anything from you until you can show me a divorce decree."

I stepped back and slammed my door, then went back to watching TV and eating my ice cream. And I have to tell you, I left that job after all of that drama. I was too embarrassed to stay. It took a quick minute for me to start another job too.

Sista E

Women, why do we eat ice cream when we are sad? When we go through a breakup, the first thing we grab is a pint of ice cream. I find that funny.

CHAPTER 6

Oatmeal Cookies and Me

It was time for school to let out for the summer. A friend of mine from college had called me and said, "Hey, Butler Street is looking for a program coordinator. Are you on the market?"

I was like, "Yes, sure, why not?" I enjoyed my time with the babies last summer, and as the summer began, parents would need summer camps. They needed me to set up the programs and run them along with after-school programs and literacy programs for the community. I absolutely loved this idea. I began creating programs and marketing for those programs. I threw myself into my work. Working a lot helped me forget what I was going through with the breakup. It was a job I could be proud of.

I soon became passionate and engulfed in my work. June 5th came, and I was working at the front desk for summer registration. I remember my head was down, and I was writing something. I heard the door open, but I didn't look up right away.

I said, "Good morning," as they walked over to me, although my head was still down.

In reply, I heard this deep Barry-White voice say, "Good morning. I need information on your summer programs." I instantly lifted my head to see this tall, bald, caramel-chocolate, nicely thick man and was immediately so mesmerized that I forgot what I was doing and where I was until I heard these two adorable little boys say hi.

I stood up and shook their hands. "What are your names?"

Sista E

They responded with a smile, and I was immediately immensely in love. One said, "Thing One."

The other said, "And I am Thing Two, and it's my birthday."

And then Tall, Bald and Nicely Thick said, "I'm their father, Mr. Camry."

I gave Mr. Camry information on the summer camp programs and said that if he liked, the boys could start right away. I gave Thing Two some candy and wished him a happy birthday. I gave them a tour around the building while explaining our different programs. The boys would start camp the next day.

I was so excited to see them the next morning—each of them. I smiled entirely too big as they came through the door. The youngest of the three ran up and hugged me. I was shocked, but I took that hug. I think he was bribing me for more candy; it was a setup.

As Dad turned to take off, I said, "I'll take good care of them while you're away. Enjoy your day."

"You promise?"

"I never make a promise I cannot keep. Yes, I promise."

He winked and went on out the door.

Now remember I was just getting over a heartbreak, so I wasn't taking that flirting too far. But I recognized it as flirting, so that was a start to show I was getting over Mr. Bus Driver.

I showed Thing One and Thing Two to their rooms, where they would start their camp day. I went on to working and doing the things I did.

Hours later, Thing Two found his way into my office before that day was over. His stomach was hurting. I asked a series of questions that led me to feeding him. Funny how a little food will make growing boys all better.

> *In my defense, Thing One and Thing Two were some really adorable little boys, and I was in love on sight with them. So yes, I can admit it now; they had me wrapped around their fingers from hello.*

I made my rounds for the day, and Thing One wanted to follow me around. He wanted to know what I did all day, so, I showed him

Now, this summer camp had a hundred and thirty campers and twenty junior staff campers. I was responsible for all one hundred and fifty kids. The junior campers were teenagers fourteen to sixteen who had summer jobs, and the campers were schoolchildren aged five to twelve. I also had some great adult assistants, so I wasn't at it alone.

As the summer progressed, Thing One and Thing Two and I formed a bond. Father's Day was approaching, and Thing One and Thing Two came into the camp like they always did and came straight into my office as if they owned the place. But this day, they weren't their usual chipper selfies.

I asked what was wrong, and they said, "Our dad's birthday is this weekend, and so is Father's Day, and we don't know what to do."

"Oh really?"

Now, let's pause a minute and back up. Mr. Camry and I spoke every day since day one. We held long, extensive conversations each evening when he picked up the boys. It usually started with the boys' behavior in the camp that day and would soon progress into how my day was or how his day was or just a little bit more important stuff about himself and me.

Okay, where were we? Right. Celebrations.

The boys looked really sad about not getting their handsome and sexy daddy a gift. I said, "Well, that's easy. I can help with this." Yup even the little guys would easily get me to do their work for them—charming at a young age.

On my lunch break, I ran to Underground Atlanta. I grabbed a beautiful, loving birthday card and Father's Day card, plus a Masonic t-shirt. I put it in a gift bag and said, "Okay, guys, give this to Dad this weekend."

Thing One asked, "How did you know what to get him?"

"I guessed."

He said, "My dad has a picture like this t-shirt on his wall."

The day would soon be over, and when Mr. Camry picked them up, I said, "So tell me more about this picture on your wall at home."

"How did you know about my picture?"

"A little birdie told me."

"Well, how about you come over, and I can show it to you in person."

My jaw hit the floor, my panties got wet, and I began to daydream immediately and forgot he was still standing there in front of me. When I came back to reality, I said, "Yes, sure." He gave me his number and said for me to call him. I took it and was still smiling ear to ear.

The weekend came and went, and I didn't call him. Monday came around quickly, and the boys were back at the camp. I asked the boys how the weekend was, and they were excited and said, "My dad really liked his gifts."

Dad would later come in to pick the boys up, and he came into my office. "Thank you. I know it was you."

"I haven't a clue what you speak of." I was sworn to secrecy.

We laughed, and he said, "Allow me to properly thank you. Come over and hang out with us." Needless to say, a man that fine, you don't make him ask a third time. I went over, and that began a new friendship. Mr. Camry and I would talk for hours. We didn't have sex. We just talked and talked and talked. We talked about everything. He was a Mason, and I was an Eastern Star, and we talked about everything under the sun. Our conversations would come so easily. He held my attention; he intrigued me. This man was a complete package deal. He was definitely a dream guy.

He was single, employed with benefits, and had three boys that he had custody of. Yup, he was a single dad. He attended church regularly. He was a trustee and a deacon in his church, and he was fine—bald head and tall, just how I liked them! And did I mention this man was fine, fine?

He and I would speak frequently. I visited regularly. I remember a time there was a conflict among the kids in our seven-to-eight-year-old group at the camp. I went, sat the group down, and we talked about conflict resolution without violence.

I had just finished one of my hearty speeches, and I heard one little boy say, "Ms. Emori likes me because she talks to me all the time."

Well, Thing Two said, "She doesn't like you more than she likes me because I saw her yesterday."

The other little boy said, "Ugh, no, you didn't. Yesterday was Sunday."

Thing Two said, "I know because she was at my house."

My head turned so quickly to this conversation. "Okay, fellas, let's talk about the weather or candy or shoes." In my mind, I was like, *Anything, but Ms. Emori was at my house yesterday.* If I could have turned colors, I would have.

I later pulled Thing One and Thing Two aside and said, "What we do away from here, we don't discuss up here."

Thing Two said just as loudly as a seven-year-old could, "But you were at our house yesterday."

Thing One hit his brother and said, "Shut up, dummy. She doesn't want everybody to know she likes our daddy."

Again, if I could turn colors, I would have. I put my hand over my face and just shook my head, laughing. Laughing was the only thing I could do.

Later, Dad picked them up, and I gave him the day's rundown. This man laughed so hard you would have thought we were at a Cocoa Brown comedy show. I asked him what was so funny.

"That my son recognizes that you like me." I put my head down, shaking it and laughing. Yes, at this point, I was blushing.

He said, "Well, do you?"

"You all right, I guess."

He then asked me to help him study. He was studying a level I had already accomplished, and he claimed he needed a study partner. I asked him why he needed my help.

"Because you're beautiful and smart. Your intelligence surpasses many women I have known, and it will give me an opportunity to get to know you better."

Now, if you know like I know, then you know that was the panty-dropping line given at every rite of passage to be used on women of all ages.

I smiled at him and said, "Let me think about it. Let me check my calendar and get back to you." Of course, later, I said yes.

The summer would continue, and if we were not talking on the phone at night, I was at his place. I would soon be wrapped up in this man. I was so intrigued by him. His knowledge and his conversations captivated me. I admired this man.

I was never one of those easy to impress kind of girls. It took more than flashing money at me to make me smile. It was more than wining and dining with me. It took more than sex to impress me. I was an independent woman. I was young, but I was a mover and a shaker. So not just every man I met couldn't get the time of day with me. There had to be something unique about him. And even then, if he was lucky enough to get an audience with me, it was even harder to hold my attention.

This man was the first man I had ever admired. I wasn't raised with my biological father. I had an older brother, a stepfather, and a grandpa. But they worked all the time. So, my first view of men was that they were workaholics. My brother was always at a church function or playing music. He was a musician. My stepdad was always working. So, you had to be a mover and shaker to get my attention; that's all I knew of men.

But there was something different about this man. It wasn't just his looks, although he was fine for sure. But his personality was impressive too. He was the first man I had known who was a single father—a man who actually had custody of his kids. I was in awe as that wasn't normal. Normally, women had their own kids, and men were the noncustodial parent.

The biggest kicker for me with this guy was, we didn't jump right into bed—well, not right away. We would spend time together so much that he would trust me with his boys. I would grab his boys and take them to the movies—just me and the kids. It wasn't like he needed me to babysit. I enjoyed hanging out with the boys. I remember one movie we saw together was *Remember the Titans*. We went to Magic Johnson's theater to see that movie, and we had a ball.

As the summer wound down, our camp put on an end of the summer program. The seven and eight-year-old boys decided to redo a scene from the movie *Major Payne*. Thing Two pretended he was the little boy from the movie, and he had the spotlight role. But he literally got nervous, and me being me, I did what I could to make him feel comfortable. He ran and hugged me so big after the performance that Mr. Camry had to take notice.

Mr. Camry would tell me later that that hug was what caught his attention about me. After that program was over, the camp ended. Mr. Camry said he was dropping the kids off at their mother's place and wanted to know what I was doing later.

"The girls and I are going to go hang out." "Oh really? A few of the guys and I are going to Dungeons on Ponce. Y'all should stop through."

"We might. Nothing guaranteed but a possibility."

It was August 4th, a Friday night, and my BFF was preparing to elope with this weird guy back in Milwaukee, Wisconsin, and I wasn't there to participate. So going to hang out and drink a little something something was the move for me. I remember staying late at the camp and calling a few friends to meet me at Dungeons.

I went on over, and yup, as soon as I walked in, I saw him and his friend sitting at the bar. I went over and said hi on my way toward the bathroom. He introduced me to his friend, and they said, "Join us until your friends get here."

I did, and Mr. Camry immediately asked me what was I drinking. He and his friend were laughing and having a good ole time while I was just as nervous as I could be.

I asked him, "What are y'all drinking because y'all look like y'all are having too much fun."

He said, "Okay, bartender, get her an Oatmeal Cookie."

Now I'm a fat girl. I love cookies. Little did I know Oatmeal Cookie wasn't a cookie at all. Yes, they laughed at me. I was wondering why the bartender looked at me with a smirk and he only asked for a cookie. Well, that dang-on oatmeal cookie had me off my feet and my legs in the air. It was a drink, and the drink was called Oatmeal Cookie.

Let me go back a moment. I'm not a drinker, never have been. I liked fruity drinks or sweet drinks, and as you can see, I was super happy about a cookie. Well, that darn cookie had a slow grind to it. And when it hit, it hit!

This man was also drunk; he had a few too many. Needless to say, my homegirls never showed up. I asked him, a drunk, to take me home. Yeah, well, he couldn't drive; and neither could I. But I love the responsible man he was. He said, "I'm too intoxicated to drive either of us home. But we can walk down to my guy's place and sober up, and I'll get you home afterward." I agreed.

Well, on this walk, we were laughing and talking, and I almost fell. And he caught me. He held my hand all the way to his friend's place. It was a two-block walk that felt like an eternity. We got there, and his friend immediately went and crashed on his bed. Mr. Camry and I fell onto the couch. We were trying to talk and then passed out. I remember waking up at o-dark-early, trying to stand up, still a little intoxicated, and Mr. Camry pulled me back into his arms and kissed me. Now I tried pulling away, and he kissed me again. I looked at him.

He paused and asked, "Do you want me to stop?"

"Nope." And I kissed him back.

Needless to say, a chance meeting on June 5th ended with us sleeping together on his friend's couch on August 4th—well, 5th because it was well past midnight. Who would have guessed it?

Now I had dreams of sliding down that tall, handsome tree since the first day he said hi. But to actually feel him inside of me, well, that was another story. I would always make jokes with one of my friends who worked with me at the camp. I would tell her, "I just want to climb that tall stalk and slide right on down." But remember now, he was a man I had come to respect and admire. I had put him on this pedestal, and I couldn't see past that admiration. I felt like I had achieved a goal. To sleep with this fine older established man—yeah, I was walking on cloud nine, and you couldn't tell me nothing. This was my man, and I knew it. Well, we had not said it, but it felt like it. Still, I played it cool, calm and collected.

The summer camp was over, and it was time for the after-school programming to begin. I became engulfed in my work again. I had not spoken to Mr. Camry for a few weeks. He called me at work, and we talked for a moment. He told me he had a show to do and invited me and one of my friends.

We went to his show, and I got to see him in action. He stepped and danced, and it was really cute to see him in his environment. We continued to talk as the months went by. We didn't have a lot of sex. I was busy, and school had started for the boys. So, we didn't see each other much, but we made time to talk a lot over the telephone. It was like we had sex once or twice a month. Sex wasn't a big part of us. It was great when we did, but it wasn't at the forefront for us. And I liked that. It was almost as if I was doing it the proper way this time, like I would get God's blessing for keeping my legs closed a little more often. Haha! As if that's how God works.

> Many people believe they can bargain their way into heaven like "God, if I do this, then you can do that." You can't bargain your way into the pearly gates. You do have to believe in Him and His promises, but that's another book at another time.

Months later, I'm thinking, *Okay, I want more. I want to give us a title.* So, I asked him about us being a thing.

He said, "I don't know. We're still just getting to know each other."

"Okay, we'll give it a little more time. After all, we just met in June, and it's only October."

> Ladies, if he doesn't at the very least know if he wants to date you exclusively after five months, he's just not that into you. And you need to pay attention to your clues and intuition. The signs are there. We are just too "dickmatized" to accept them. We continue to push the envelope, and then we get hurt, and now we're mad at the world.

As the holidays approached going into November, he and I were seeing each other more and more. We were talking about dreams and what we wanted to accomplish in this life. I would talk to him about opening up a group home in Atlanta for troubled youth. He would give me great ideas. I remember he called me once, and we were talking and laughing over the telephone, and he told me the boys were going to their moms for the weekend.

I was like "Oh, that's good." I had missed him, and I wanted to see him. So, the next day I got up early, stopped at Waffle House and picked up a steak-and-egg breakfast, then drove to Mr. Camry's place.

Now I had just spoken with him the night before, so I knew he would be home. I popped up at his house wearing a French coat and high heels. Yep, you guessed it, nothing else underneath that coat but drawls and titties. I was planning a breakfast date like none other.

> If done correctly, this makes for a really good night with a man, and it definitely goes a long way in his memory.

So, I was at his door with a Waffle House breakfast in one hand and holding my French coat in the other. I rang the doorbell, he opened it, and I said, "Good morning, handsome. Here's breakfast." I handed him the Waffle House and then added, "And here's an early dessert." And I opened my coat. He was smiling ear to ear. But then I heard something in his background and quickly closed my coat.

"Honey, you are not alone."

"Nope." And then I saw it was the boys.

Again, I was mortified, and I asked him, "What happened to the kids leaving for the weekend yesterday?"

He said their mother didn't come to get them last night. "We're on the way out the door to drop them off."

"Why didn't you tell me that before I opened my coat?"

Now he was laughing. He said to the boys, "Come give Ms. Emori a hug."

My eyes were lit up like a Christmas tree. "No, boys, just say hi. And I'll see you guys later," I said as I was trying to move fast off that porch back to my car.

Mr. Camry was still laughing as I tried to get off that porch. I had no more clothes with me. I couldn't let the boys see my birthday suit that was planned strictly for Daddy's dessert.

I finally left and went home, and I admit, I was laughing all the way. I had almost exposed a seven and eight-year-old to the world of titties.

I was trying to be a good girl with this guy. He was the first man who had impressed me. He was a godly man and a family man. He had a legal job and no hidden wife. He loved his momma, and his shoes were big. He was fine as all getup. His conversations held my attention, and I enjoyed being with him. I enjoyed having conversations with him. Everything about this man was perfect. I was falling for him and hard.

All the while, I was working on opening a group home for troubled kids. I told him I loved his ideas and would love to have him be part of my board of directors. Around this time, he mentioned to me we couldn't have a business relationship and a personal relationship. He said I had to choose one. He said he couldn't mix business with pleasure and could only do one or the other.

Now he did call me back later that day after he got home from dropping the boys off. I came back over, this time with clothes on and dessert covered up. The night was amazing. We watched a movie and had sex. Well, we attempted to have sex. As we were processing slowly into motion, the condom broke. Lawd, why did the condom break before we completed our tasks? No more condoms were around either. Needless to say, we had used them all up. So, I rolled over and fell asleep.

A while later, I woke up with this man on top of me doing his dang-on thang. Yes, honey, I woke up for that treat. I was very happy to reach the finish line with his smiling face. He rolled over and fell immediately to sleep. I must admit your girl put in good work once I finally woke up.

Now we know what happens when you have sex without a condom. And I'll be damned, but at the time, I was not thinking about whether I could end up pregnant or contract a sexually transmitted disease. The condom broke, I went to sleep. I woke up in action (and it was good action), so I went with the moment. Not a second thought went to the consequences of my feel-good actions. He liked me, and I liked him. It was go time.

Later the next day or so, he brought up the relationship conversation. He made mention of why he thought mixing business and personal wouldn't work. Well in my mind, business and personal did mix. Who wouldn't want to have the person they loved and trusted, whom they were lovers with, go into a partnership in business?

We discussed why he didn't want to and how it would fail and break down the relationship. I totally disagreed with his opinion and said, "Well, if I have to choose, I'm always going to choose money over love." My mindset at the time was, love can't pay no bills, and sex ends at midnight. Therefore, I'm choosing money every time. I choose business over personal. He didn't seem to like my answer as he reiterated my choice. I confirmed it with a full attitude like, "Yes, that's what I said."

He finally said okay.

After that conversation, it seemed as if we started to drift apart. We didn't talk as much, nor did we see each other that much. The last time we saw each other was on December 9th. He came over to my place, and we watched the premiere of Terry McMillian's *Disappearing Acts* together. We had talked about the book a time before, and now to watch the movie was the icing on the cake. But we didn't have sex that night. We really didn't talk much after that.

Summer camp was over, and the school year had long since begun. So I wouldn't see the boys as much either. As I began to think, I felt like it was just a summer fling that went into the fall and ended as the winter began to break.

Now here is where it began to get tricky. I saw Mr. Bus Driver in passing, and I waved at him and kept going. He was working, driving a new route down Buford Highway. I was shocked to see him, as we were nowhere near his normal route or my place of residence.

I stopped and said hi, and he asked how I was doing. "I'm keeping busy working at Butler Street and enjoying working with the kids."

"Oh yeah? Well, you're looking good, I see."

"Thank you, and have a nice day." I left the scene before I fell for his quick wit and good looks. This was the end of September.

Well, Mr. Bus Driver appeared at my job the following week. He just popped up—no call, no page, no heads-up. He just showed up. Y'all, it was my Mr. Bus Driver. Yep, I slept with him. We went back to my place and talked briefly, and I told him don't come back until he had a divorce decree in his hands.

So here I was with the end of the year coming up, and no Mr. Camry. He and I decided to be business partners only. And No Mr. Bus Driver either because he decided to lie about being married. What a year it had been. I couldn't really complain because it had been a year of growth and heartbreak but growth nonetheless.

> The most important lesson I learned was the most dangerous creature on this earth is a woman. She can destroy a king or a kingdom. See Delilah in the Bible. But only smart men know how powerful women really are. See Boaz in the Bible. What we have to remember is that we are the prize, the favor that God intended as in (Proverbs

> 18:22). We cannot allow these men to make
> us feel less than what God created us to be.

It was now mid-December. I had received a telephone call from Mr. Bus Driver. I, of course, invited him over to my place. We hung out a bit. He told me he was applying for a divorce. I guess in my mind that was good enough. Still, I didn't sleep with him—well, not that time anyway.

The Butler Street job had slowed down, and now I had started working for the city. I was working in the projects (Grady Homes, Thela Heights) assisting women on welfare. I was working on the W-2 program and assisting women who wanted to finish high school or get their GED, helping them with resume building and getting a job. Yes, it was kind of cool. But once Mr. Bus Driver found out about my new job, he was concerned.

He was concerned because he had grown up in Bankhead Courts, and he knew I was from Milwaukee, Wisconsin, which he called the Valley. He was concerned folks would scare me away. So much so that he changed his work schedule to take me to work and pick me up.

Listen, I thought the hoods of Milwaukee streets were bad, but nope, I wasn't that tough. I was put at a site where they would shoot and rob you in the daytime and not think twice. Heck, they didn't think once. But it was my job, and it was in my field. I was doing social work. I was helping families to become self-sufficient.

This would have Mr. Bus Driver and me closer again. One weekend I was sick and couldn't get out of bed. Mr. Bus Driver brought me some soup and was there trying to help me feel better. I was not a girl who got sick often, and this sickness lasted too long. So long that I had to take off work from my new job. I knew then if I had to take off work, something major had to be wrong with me.

I ended up going to the Southside Clinic because I didn't have any insurance yet with my job. This was a state-run clinic that helped people with no insurance. They had student doctors and a lot of college students as patients. Well, my cousin had been to the clinic a few weeks before me, and they sent her home and told her she had a sexually transmitted disease—yes, an STD. She ended up in Grady Memorial a week later to find out she didn't have an STD but a fetus. So needless to say, this made me nervous that these folks didn't half know what they were doing over here. But where else could I go? I had no insurance, and I was sick and had taken off of work.

I went on in the door of the clinic. It was packed. At this point, I didn't care. I just need medicine so I could get back to work the next day.

Well, the doctor came in, he listened to my symptoms (vomiting, dizziness, not able to keep food down, headaches), and he immediately ordered a pregnancy test.

I got plum ignat, flat-out going way off. "Why is it because I'm young and Black the first thing you go to is I'm pregnant? I'm an educated working woman. Just because I'm young and Black doesn't mean I'm pregnant. You need to check for something else. You diagnosed my cousin with an STD, and it turns out she's pregnant. So now you wanna test me for pregnancy? I just don't think you people know what you're doing here."

He said, "Ma'am, your test came back. You *are* pregnant."

My mouth hit the floor in shock with boldness and assurance. "Sir, you're going to need to redo that test. That test was inconclusive."

He looked me in my eyes. "No, it wasn't inconclusive. It was definitive. But if it will make you happier, we'll run a blood test. By the way, ma'am, when was your last period?"

Yes, he shut my mouth quickly. I was clueless when my last menstrual cycle was. "Well, my cycles are irregular and have been since I was a teen. I would need to check my calendar when I get home to give you a direct answer."

"That's fine. I'll schedule you an ultrasound so we can better tell."

I looked at the calendar he had on the wall. "I think my last period was September."

He said with a smirk on his face, "It's December, ma'am. Do you still want me to go ahead with the blood test?"

"Excuse you, sir, but yes, I do. I don't believe I'm pregnant. It's impossible!"

"Well, ma'am, do you have sex?" Keep in mind he had this look of smugness on his face, and I had a look of disbelief.

"Yes, sir, I do have sex. But it's always protected, and it's been a while ago."

He then got technical on me. "Birth control is only ninety-eight percent effective and depending on which one."

I stopped that man in his tracks and yelled, "Just go get the damn test!"

He's practically laughing at me by this time. "The nurse will be right in to draw your blood and give you a follow-up appointment."

Sista E

A short time later the nurse came in and said, "Well, according to your last menstrual cycle, you would be nine or ten weeks pregnant. You should start taking these, and here's your next appointment after the holidays."

"Holidays? What holiday?" My mind was running as I was starting to cry. *I cannot be pregnant. My momma is gonna kill me. No, wait, my grandma told me to keep my legs closed and my drawls up. I'm the preacher's kid. I can't be pregnant. Lawd, how am I pregnant? That's impossible. I haven't been doing nobody up. Well, in a little long while. Well, maybe I have, but...*

The thoughts were running through my head, and the tears were flowing down my face. I left there in straight disbelief. This was impossible. I was a godmomma. I could take those kids home but I could not keep a kid.

Then as I got home, I looked at my personal calendar.

> Y'all remember when you wrote initials in your personal calendar? You had the stars that represented the days you were on your period, then you had those initials on there like SWL and circled it if you had on a condom and crossed it out if there was problems with the condoms. But S was sex, W was with, and L was the first initial of the name of who it was. Yeah, don't act. I wasn't the only one tracking who I spread my legs with. We're great at record-keeping for incidents just like this!

Well, I got home, opened up my personal calendar, went back to the last star on my book, and then I looked for those SW initials. And lo and behold, SWBD was there. Yup, "Sex with Mr. Bus Driver" was sitting right there with a big ole smiley face with a long cross-out. Yup, you guessed it, condom issues.

I started crying and crying, screaming, "What have I done? This man is still married." The personal calendar took me back to that time he popped up at my job after I saw him on his new bus route. That one time, I slept with him because I was stressed out and horny.

Now, I knew my momma would kill me. I was pregnant, and by a married man. I went to sleep and paged him. Why did I just page this man?

He's still married, he hasn't responded, and it's hours later. Finally, I just fell asleep.

Who but who popped up the next morning? I opened the door and went to lie back down. Now I was depressed and not only pregnant but pregnant by a married man. I felt like God was punishing me.

Back at home, my little sister was pregnant at 19, and I had fussed at her—*interesting how folks will ridicule you for doing the same thing they're doing in secret*—and my brother and his wife had announced at Thanksgiving that they were pregnant. Wait, remember my cousin who had a misdiagnosis just two weeks prior? She was officially pregnant too. And now here I was, bringing shame to my family. I wasn't married. I wasn't a teen, and now I was pregnant by a married man. I wasn't even in a relationship with hopes of getting married.

Sista E

Mr. Bus Driver came in and asked if I was feeling better. I said no and ran to lie back down. He followed me and said, "What's wrong? I thought you went to the doctor yesterday. What did the doctor say?"

"The dumb doctor doesn't know what he's talking about." Yes, I was still in my feelings y'all.

"Okay, what did he say?" he asked, as he laid down on my bed.

I straddled him and looked him in his eyes. "The doctor said I'm pregnant with your child."

Mr. Bus Driver looked at me like he had just seen a ghost. He was too dark to turn colors, but if he could have turned colors he would have. After his moment of silence, he asked, "Well, what are you going to do?"

> Men, don't ever ask her what she is going to do. Always speak French. It was "we, we, we" when you were having fun. It needs to be "we, we, we" when we're in trouble. Even though it is ultimately her decision, saying we makes it a little less frightening.

So, when Mr. Bus Driver asked me what I was going to do, I exploded. "What the hell do you mean what am *I* going to do?" I was screaming and beating him in his chest. Then I jumped all on the bed, yelling and crying, "My life is over. My life is over, and all you can do is ask what am I going to do?" I acted a plum fool. So much so I scared both of us.

My follow-up appointment was almost a month later. I went to my appointment, and wouldn't you believe I got the same smug doctor who came in and made it clear that my blood and urine test both stated that I was pregnant. He showed both results to me. I sat there, and I didn't say a word. Yes, I had to eat humble pie and close my mouth.

Then the x-ray tech came in to complete the ultrasound. I was talking to the tech, and he was like, "Yes, I understand sometimes we do get a false reading on pregnancy tests." That's usually when they would get a blood test. But I was now talking to this tech about my experience here while he's working. And then he said, "Well, looks like you are about eight weeks, and your due date should be on or around August 13th."

"Wait a minute, when I was here last they said I was about nine or ten weeks. How did we go backward? Wait, that can't be right."

"Yes, I'm looking at the fetus, and those measurements are correct. This means you would have gotten pregnant around the 19th of November."

I screamed, "No no no no, this can't be happening to me."

He was like, "What? What's wrong? You told the wrong man you're pregnant?" and started to laugh like he was just playing, trying to be funny.

"Yes. While you're playing, I did tell the wrong person. But wait, who was I with in November?" I pulled out my personal calendar. Yes, I remembered to bring it with me this time. I opened the book and saw SWC—yep, "Sex with Mr. Camry." I laughed so hard so much so the tech laughed too. I started to just laugh and shake my head, then tears started to fall. The last real conversation he and I had was about me choosing business. I hadn't talked to him too much after that.

Mr. Camry had been blowing me off. He wasn't really taking my calls after I chose business over personal. Little did I know he had started talking to one of his son's school teachers and had started dating her. Now we would have conversations about Thing One acting out in school. That poor baby was just trying to get his daddy's attention. He had been acting out in summer camp, but I handled it differently than what the school teacher had. Well, apparently the school teacher was busy trying to get Daddy's attention and not help this student overcome his issues and she certainly had accomplished getting Daddy's attention.

When I popped at his place because he really hadn't taken my calls, he came to the door and said, "Hey, what's up?" Then he came out on the porch, not inviting me in as he usually did. No, he came out on the porch. Yup, clue number one. Something was not right.

So now my attitude grew. I said, "I've been trying to reach you."

"Well, I've been busy."

Women, when he starts his reason with an excuse, just know he's trying to save face. He doesn't want to admit it, but it's another woman.

I said, "Well, you could have found some time if you wanted to."

"What's up, sweetheart?" He would always call me sweetheart even still to this day.

"Look we need to talk."

"Talk."

"I'm pregnant." He stepped back. "And before you make the mistake of asking by who, it's yours. I just had an ultrasound, and it puts me back to the night I delivered Waffle House for breakfast and came back later that night."

His first words were, "Damn. How am I gonna tell her this now?"

"Uhm, excuse me, sir? What? You're more concerned about another woman than me at this moment?" Well, instead of me acting a plum fool again, I walked off, got in my car, and left as he was calling my name. I didn't pause to even look back.

I kept going and started crying. In a month, I had learned I was pregnant and had now told two men I was pregnant and claimed that both were the father.

> Why do we open our mouths before we are even sure, knowing we've slept with multiple people? And why do we then get so upset at the guys for them questioning in disbelief? They know they've been with multiple women as well. But we go to the tenth degree because this man questioned you about the paternity.

Mr. Camry called me the next day. He told me he had started seeing the school teacher, and she was the one at his place when I came by. Mr. Camry now wanted to know what my plans were for this pregnancy. I told him I didn't know yet, but I did know I was keeping my baby. He said he had three kids already and a strong possibility of one more. Then he proceeded to throw in my face that I chose a business relationship over a personal relationship. He also stated that I had trapped him.

> Now, you know, like I know, saying a woman trapping a man is fighting words. Whether it's true or not, it's about to be some problems.

I completely lost the cool I had with him. I explained to him how he's broke with three and possibly another kid already, and he lived in some apartments, not a house, but apartments on Simpson Road. I asked him now that if I was going to trap a man, wouldn't I at least trap a man with more money and fewer kids. Now let's think about that.

He got quiet, and I hung up. It would be months later before I spoke with him again.

In the meantime, I had to call Mr. Bus Driver. Yup, I was woman enough to call him to correct my mistake. I asked him to come over for dinner after work. He agreed. How many of you know that a way to a man's heart is through his stomach? At least that's what the old folks taught us. So, I figured if I was about to break his heart, I might as well fill his stomach.

He came over, and dinner wasn't quite ready. I had candles lit and some Anita Baker playing. The atmosphere was just right. The food had the place smelling just right, plus my candles were great.

I, of course, seduced him not soon after he walked in the door. You better believe I put it on him too, laid him down on the bed, and began kissing him from head to toe. Yes, I made him say my name while the food was cooking.

As soon as the food was done, I fixed his plate and made him feel like a king. Then round two was dessert, and I was on the menu. I fed him strawberries. I placed the strawberry on top of me as I lay down. As soon as he was done, I laid him down on the bed on his back and straddled him again. This time, our clothes were completely off. Yep, we're in our birthday suits. You know this is when the cuddling starts. But I wasn't a cuddler. I didn't like to be held; that was too intimate for me. And I definitely didn't kiss. *Pretty Woman* told me that makes it personal.

Well, this day, I cuddled and kissed and then told him this baby wasn't his. We laid there quiet and still. He didn't move, so I didn't move. I didn't say anything else. I was quiet as a church mouse. I wanted to let him process and act up if he needed to since I had acted up previously myself. So, I was ready for his scene, and there would be nothing I could say. But he didn't.

He remained calm and cool. I thought his staying calm and cool scared me because I knew I would have been pissed. Hell, I was upset for him. But he just ended the night and left. As he was leaving, he asked, "How do you know?"

"They did the ultrasound, and it showed my exact date versus the date according to my last menstrual cycle, which is what they did at first and why I thought it was yours. The doctors kept saying to count from my last period. And from my last period, it was you I had slept with when you came up to my job. I'm sorry.

He looked at me and walked out the door.

CHAPTER 7

So, You're Pregnant. Now What?

*Woman to woman—***Shirley and Barbara, Monica and Brandy, Fantasia and Jennifer...**
Yep, they've written song after song, hit after hit, about women fighting over a man. What we cannot keep doing is fighting over a man.
That man does not belong to you.
He lied to you.
She probably is right.
In one moment, in a blink of an eye, you could be in her shoes.
Men will keep sucking the life outta you, and you keep giving him the straw. The love you're looking for, whatever you're looking for, ain't coming from no man; it's coming from The Man—The Man up above.

The season of pregnant and alone would be my song. I was scared and wasn't sure about the future. Sure, I had been a great godmother and a great sister-mom, but now it would be just Mom. And everything this kid would ever need would fall on me.

The old saying goes, "Momma's baby, Papa's maybe." Well, true story. Mom, it is definitely your responsibility, and maybe Daddy will be there and maybe he won't. But you, my dear, will have to figure this thing out. So, I did what any reasonable fresh outta college kid would do. I ran home to my mommy. But before that…

My pregnancy had become high risk, and I was sick all the time, driving down Peachtree Road, throwing up from whatever I had just smelled. When April came, I finally called Mr. Camry and asked for a meeting. We met up at Dungeon. We hadn't spoken since the day I told him I was pregnant on his porch. I didn't want to be like the last person and just disappear with his kid and leave him not knowing.

I warned him, "Hey, I don't really look that pregnant, but there is a little person kicking around inside of me for sure."

We met up, and he looked at me and said, "Oh no, you look pregnant all right." That made both of us laugh and broke the ice.

"I'm about to go home to my momma. I'm not asking you for anything. Just letting you know in case I don't come back to Atlanta."

"I want to get to know my kid." We began to go over particulars like names.

"The baby will have my name. We aren't married."

"Well, if it's my child, I want him to have my name." We ended the conversation about names, and he reminded me that I chose business over personal.

"Gee, thanks." I left there and went to my cousin's place. We were hanging out, and I got sick. Sick, sick, sick. She took me to the hospital. We thought I was in early labor or something.

She said, "You need to call the father and tell him."

"No, I'm good. He doesn't need to know anything."

Let's just say my cousin was a bully, and I later did exactly what she said. He didn't answer, so I left a voicemail. A few

Sista E

moments later, I got a return call. Yup, that darn star sixty-nine gets folks in trouble a lot.

My cousin answered the phone. I was lying in the hospital bed. I heard my cousin say, "This is who?" with a look of concern on her face.

I reached for the phone and said, "Hello, who is this?"

"It's the schoolteacher, Mr. Camry's wife."

I then sat up quickly. She now had my full attention. I asked her, "What do you mean 'wife'?"

"Yes, we got married last week. Well, who exactly are you?"

"I'm Emori, and I'm carrying his baby and have been for the last seven months."

"Well, Mr. Camry told me you were his Eastern Star sister, and there was nothing between y'all."

"Well, I'm glad he told you that because his dick was between us, and now nine months later, a baby comes out. So, if you don't mind, this call was for him, not you. Please have him call me when he returns."

She was now in her feelings and wanted to ask too many questions.

I redirect her back to him.

"He said it's not his child, and I don't want you to call this house again."

> Now we all know there are always two sides to every story, and then there's the truth. So, Sis, if you don't have both sides of the story, hold your horses and learn the truth. We know anything and everything done

> in the dark will always come to light; just be patient. The truth will surface, and even then, you should ease your way into that situation.
>
> Why? Because at any given moment, you could be her, or you were once her. But humble yourself, and don't think you're better than her just because you're sucking on the dick today and he's smiling in your face. You don't really know what happened between that man and that woman despite what he told you.

He would soon get home and call me. He asked what was wrong. But I ignored everything he was saying. I had a question of my own. "Did the school teacher just say 'wife'? Did you just marry another woman while I'm seven months pregnant carrying your child?"

"You chose business—"

I hung up before he could finish his statement. For me, not answering the question was the answer.

Mr. Camry continued to live his life on honeymoon mode. The school teacher made him change his number, and the only way I could reach him after that was to contact him at work.

I left for Milwaukee with my emotions all over the place. The only thing I could think of was I was pregnant by a married man. I was alone, lost, and confused while heading home to my momma's house.

My momma used to always make a joke like, "I sent you to college to get a husband." I knew it was a joke, but it stayed in the back of my mind.

> *How many of you know every joke has some truth?*

So here I was, back at my momma's house with a baby on the way—no job, no man, just bills and a baby. To my surprise, my parents received me with open arms and genuine love. Actually, it wasn't surprising; that's just how my family is. They won't judge you. They might talk about you and make fun of you, but no judgment. I actually can't recall them ever asking about the daddy. I had added extra worry to my life for no reason.

As time went on, I had a conversation with my grandma, who said, "Daddies aren't important. This baby is going to need all the strength God has given you and then some. But I believe you can do this. You have been a fighter since you entered this world. Don't let having this baby unwed stop you now." My grandma was a beast at womanhood. I low-key think she was a feminist.

I began to tell her about him. I remember saying, "I just don't want my baby to have their trademark chin." Mr. Camry and each of his boys had a dimple in their chin. It wasn't bad-looking; I just didn't want my baby to have it. I told my granny how much Mr. Camry wanted our baby to have his last name.

"Your baby should always have your name."

"Huh?"

"If he doesn't love you enough to give you his last name, why give the baby his name when you have to raise the baby without him? How will you explain to the baby their heritage of his last name if you don't know it? But you are clear on your heritage and where your last name came from. Give your baby you, your heritage, your legacy, your last name."

I took that to heart. Granny was a smart woman. Oh, how I miss my granny. *Rest in heaven, Flora Lee James.*

Talking with my granny gave me the strength to have my baby unwed and unashamed. I knew Mr. Camry was a crappy man for marrying someone else while I was pregnant. But that didn't stop me from emailing and professing my love for him. That didn't stop me from trying to understand why and how he chose to marry her and not me when I was the one pregnant with his child. That didn't stop my emotions from building and feelings of betrayal. I communicated with Mr. Camry more about my hurt feelings over him getting married than I did about the baby. I guess I had started to believe everything my granny had told me about my strength.

I went on to live in Milwaukee and have my baby. I birthed, by the grace of God, a healthy baby boy—ten toes, ten fingers, and yup, you guessed it, no dimple in his chinny-chin-chin. I was excited and overjoyed. The joy was big because since the day I found out I was pregnant, I was depressed and very sad. I was one step away from suicide, but no one ever knew how sad I really was.

Being pregnant was a blessing—a miracle, actually. The doctors said when I was having so many surgeries as a newborn, it would be next to impossible to have a baby. And here I was, pregnant.

But I was pregnant and unmarried—the very thing I fought so hard against when I was in college. What I didn't realize was

Sista E

I was having prepartum depression, same as postpartum, only it's before the baby is born. I would have uncontrollable crying fits. I would be sick for days, and it wasn't for medical reasons. It was mental stress.

At one point, I got so sick I was rushed to the hospital in Milwaukee by ambulance. They thought I was in labor; the pain was so intense. But it wasn't labor. The pains were real, only they had more to do with mental and emotional stress than a physical ailment, which was why the doctors couldn't diagnose what was truly wrong.

> I believe everyone should seek counseling when they first get pregnant, even if it's just once for an evaluation, because some people, like me, can hide mental and emotional pain very well. We'll mask it all while it's coming out as something else like always fussing or always angry and upset. And folks just wave it off by saying things like, "Oh, that's just her hormones." It might be, but to be on the safe side, go seek counseling. One thing for sure is, it can't hurt to speak with a professional.

I had my baby in July in Milwaukee. The delivery was scary. My baby almost died. I almost died, and, well, Mr. Camry didn't know I'd had a son until a week after the baby was born because he was off on vacation, having him a grand ole time while I was fighting for the lives of our son and me. But I do give him credit.

His fine self and great genes helped me create the most handsome, precious, and adorable baby I had ever seen.

He looked just like no one, well, at first. He was so small that I never wanted to put him down. I couldn't believe this baby was mine; this little person had lived inside me.

Now everything I had hoped for and everything I had believed would soon all go out the window. He was nothing like how I imagined him to be, nothing like I had pictured, but he was mine. He was healthy and didn't have that chin; therefore, I was good.

Labor Day weekend approached, and I wanted to go to Atlanta. I always knew I would move back to Atlanta eventually. I just needed to get my strength back. I also needed to get some money so I could take care of my baby. But somewhere in the back of my mind, I wanted to hurry up and show my baby off to Mr. Camry. For some crazy reason, I thought if I showed him our son, he would realize he'd made a mistake and leave her and marry me.

Sounds crazy, I know. Clearly, it was a crazy thought, but it was what I had fixed my mind on. It was programmed in my head that I was going to steal him back. As if he was ever mine to begin with. We had Sex, we had not made a commitment.

But let's go back to the story of Mr. Camry. Nowhere in there do I ever say I was in love with him, so why was I fascinated with getting him back? Oh, because I wanted to raise my baby with his father. Ha! That's a delusion too many women have, which is why we put up with so much BS from the man. But that's for a different part of the book; we'll come back to this.

Still, I had set my goal, and in my mind, he was the goal. I got my baby all cute and took him to Atlanta. We were scheduled to be in Atlanta for a week. I stayed at my cousin's place, and folks came over to see my baby. "Oh, he's so cute. Oh, he's a crybaby." My baby had to be about seven weeks old, so give him a break. I remember that because I had just had my six-week checkup before I went down to Atlanta.

Anyway, you know that *cat* was hot and ready to come out. And it was gone come out in Georgia. I was ready too! I even called up Mr. Bus Driver and told him I was in town and wanted to see him. His first question was, "Do you have the baby with you?"

I didn't think twice. "Yes, I got my son with me."

"I'm on my way."

I was too hyped, thinking this man was on his way to see me. I was all excited, putting on makeup getting all dolled up. My boo was on his way.

Yeah, well, he came over all right, and he just wanted to see for himself that my baby really wasn't his. Yup, pick up your crack face, honeyboo. When I realized that was the real reason he came over, I, too, had to pick up my face.

This man looked so good that I was ready to sell my soul, and he came over on a motorcycle. Girl, I was dripping wet. Now, remember I was emailing and professing my love for Mr. Camry, but now I had Mr. Bus Driver in front of me. And the thoughts that were running through my mind about what I wanted to do to Ms. Angel's baby boy were unreal.

I brought my baby outside while Mr. Bus Driver was on the bike and showed him my baby's newborn picture. He's holding my baby and looking back and forth at the picture. It was like the look of disappointment and hurt mixed in with relief.

He held my baby and asked, "What's his name?" I told him, and he said, "That's close to my momma's name."

After a minute, he gave the baby back, and I asked him to take me on a ride. He said okay, so I took my baby back in the house and asked my cousin to babysit for a moment.

> Remember me saying my seven-week-old baby was a crybaby? Shoot, he was a crybaby up until he was three years old. He had become spoiled.

My cousin was a great babysitter, and I trusted her, but she said she couldn't get him to stop crying, and so she smoked a joint with him right there. When I returned, I said, "Oh, he's sleeping so good. Thanks, Lynn. How did you do it?"

She said, "I don't even know."

Y'all, my baby smelled just like what she had been smoking. My baby had gotten a contact high from her pleasurable!

Anyway, back to my bike ride.

So, I left and went with Mr. Bus Driver on a bike ride. We didn't go anywhere special; we didn't even talk. It was the wind blowing in my face and my arms wrapped around this man. I was in awe. I wasn't thinking about my baby, and I wasn't thinking about Mr. Camry. I was only thinking about this man I was holding. He smelled good. It felt like security. It felt like safety. It felt like this was the man I was supposed to be with. The bike ride was seductive in itself. I enjoyed every bit of the moment.

He eventually returned me to my cousin's place, and when he helped me off the bike, I said, "Wow, that was amazing. Thank you."

He grabbed me and kissed the life outta me. That was one, our first kiss, and two, probably the best kiss I'd ever had. So much so that I stumbled my way back into my cousin's place. I was in love, or so I thought. I would learn later that after he left, Mr. Bus Driver was in a motorcycle accident.

The next day, Mr. Camry would come over to meet our son. I was still at my cousin's place. I had called him when we arrived, but he didn't come until two days after we got there.

He knocked on the door. I opened it. My baby was on the couch. I picked him up and said, "Here is your son," and handed him our baby.

He said, "Wow," and went and sat down with him. Mr. Camry just looked at him. He then asked me how I was doing.

"I'm good. I'm happy." We began to talk. I asked him, "Why did you marry her for real? What was your real reason?"

"You didn't want a family. I had already had my boys. You were single. It was just you."

I looked at him with tears in my eyes. "But I was carrying your child."

"It wasn't about you. It was about me. I had three kids already, and you were about to have my fourth. I didn't know what to do."

In a rage now, I yelled, "So you married her? You didn't know what to do, so your mind told you to marry another chick and not the one who was carrying your kid, someone who would take more money out of your household?"

He just put his head down and looked at our son. I walked into the kitchen to release some air. I needed to calm down so that I didn't make this an uncomfortable situation. I also needed to allow him as much time as he needed to be with his son.

When I returned, he said, "I'll start sending you money for him. Does he need anything right now?"

"Always pampers and clothes. He's growing like a wildfire."

He was still holding him and looked down again. "He looks like Thing Two."

"Yeah, I thought that too." We smiled, and time was winding up.

"Well, let me go. When are y'all leaving?"

"On the 11th at 2:00 p.m."

"Okay, I'll get back here before then."

"Okay, we'll be here." He hugged me and looked me in the eyes. "You did good work. You did good."

I stared at him with disbelief on my face. "Excuse me, what did you just say?"

He said it again, and in my mind, I was like, *Man, if you don't go and get out of here before I cuss you out… How do you tell a woman who almost died giving birth that she did good work?* All I could say was, "Good night, Mr. Camry," and close the door so quickly and so hard it was unreal.

I didn't see him again on that trip. Once I got back to Milwaukee, I talked to Mr. Camry very little as he still hadn't given me a logical reason as to why he chose to marry this woman over me. But truth be told, did he owe me an explanation?

I waited a few months before I tried reaching out to Mr. Bus Driver after my September trip to the A. And wouldn't you know, we would begin a new friendship, one that was different, one that didn't involve lies or sex. I saw the way he looked at my baby as he held him in his arms just a few months back. I remembered our intimate bike ride, and my mind just wouldn't let go of this man.

According to him, he had applied for a divorce but was still going through the process. It was now February, and I had decided to move back to the Atlanta area. I moved to Decatur this time with just me and my baby in tow, and I continued to write outlandish emails to Mr. Camry.

Every now and then, he would send money or clothes but nothing regularly. I just couldn't get over him marrying this chic over me. We would get into it often over this woman. Then I found out his boys, Thing One and Thing Two, did not like her, and she was Thing One's fourth-grade schoolteacher. He was having trouble in school, and in his mind, she was the cause.

Now, I didn't need an additional reason not to like her. She was already with the man I wanted. She was already sticking her nose in my business with this man, and now she was bothering his son. Oh, I was heated. But it wasn't my place because he wasn't my son, and Mr. Camry had interrupted my relationship with his boys. I got to see them every once in a while, but they didn't know I was pregnant with their little brother.

Mr. Camry's oldest son had been in Spain for the summer and then came back for the start of his senior year in high school. The oldest son had become very fond of my goddaughter CiCi, and he had become her close friend. They even went to prom together; they were so cute as friends. He had two loves—Toni Braxton and CiCi.

Anyway, the oldest son brought the kids to the mall so I could see the boys. I never told them I was pregnant, and Mr. Camry never told them they had a little brother. We met up at the mall, and it was good to see them. They were excited to see me but shocked I had a baby. Yet they were smart enough to ask me who the daddy was. I never alluded to them it was their dad's child. But they asked intelligent questions enough that they would soon figure it out.

Thing Two even said, "My daddy takes care of all his kids."

CiCi said, "What makes you think your daddy isn't taking care of him?"

I would listen to the stories his boys told, and I would miss them but get upset at how this schoolteacher was treating them and frustrated that I couldn't do anything about it. They weren't my kids.

One day, I called Mr. Camry, and the schoolteacher answered the phone. Of course, she and I had words.

> Never have slick words with someone who has the upper hand on you. I knew where she worked, where she lived, plus her whole name. Needless to say, I was that chick.

I pulled up to the door. She wanted me to know that she was now carrying his child and that my child wasn't his. Wrong. Big mistake Mizz Thang! Don't get in between a situation where you are only getting one side of the story.

I pulled up to his beautiful suburban home in Douglasville. Knock knock, now tell me to my face my kid isn't his. I then turned to him and said, "Better yet, since you wanna play daddy to everyone, here's another one for you."

I handed him my baby and walked off. Yes, y'all, my crazy butt dropped my baby boy off at this man's doorstep when he was ten months old. I made my statement and walked off to my car.

He called the police department. They showed up, and I was showing out. He would soon learn there was a crazy side to Ms. E, and he definitely didn't ever want to see that side of me.

Well, the police didn't care about who Ms. E was. They locked my crazy tail up and took my baby to social services. These folks had my baby for a week. I had to get bailed out of jail, I had to go to court, and then I had to show and prove I was a stable mother. And Mr. Camry, well, he got to continue with his ugly now-seven-month-pregnant wife. I did mention she was ugly, right?

So that added fuel to my fire. You chose this ugly woman over me because she was ready for a family, and I was about my money. Nope, the drama did not stop after that.

We went to court, and I was hit with a disorderly conduct charge. Mr. Camry and his beloved wife had to show up at court as well. But what upset me the most was that he gave my baby to social services. I had to have visitation with my ten-month-old spoiled baby. I had to go to the bathroom with the door open. I had to always be in his eyesight. They had drugged my baby so he would stop crying, and I was livid. They had to do a home visit on me. I didn't have much as I hadn't been back long.

When you know your mama is a rider for you, you do what I did. I called my mom and told her what happened. She took the next flight out. My mom helped get my place together for a home visit by asking the next-door neighbors—who I didn't know—if we could use their living room furniture to impress the social services people so I could get my baby back. I laughed so hard that I couldn't even be embarrassed. Later on, my soul mate, Jimmy, had a whole living room set delivered to my place in preparation.

Jimmy was always looking out for me; he had my back when I couldn't have my own.

The place looked nice, and the people came the next day to visit and to make sure I was a stable parent for my son. The judge made me and Mr. Camry go to court about our son. He brought his pregnant wife, and I brought my momma. My momma came in like a real OG. She had a look on her face that said way more than a million words could have. I wasn't sure if she was gone kill me or Mr. Camry, but when we got into the courtroom, she gave that man the death look and then told him she would beat his ass.

I was like, "Mom, you gotta calm down."

She was like, "No, he hurt my daughter and my grandson. That's a double ass-whoopin'."

"Mom, but we're in court, and I need to pretend to be nice, so I can get my baby."

She calmed down a bit, but the judge put his wife and my mother out of the courtroom. He said, "I only want to speak with the parents of this child."

Social services had already done a home visit and study on me, and they gave their report in the courtroom. The judge gave us a lecture, and I was granted my baby back and never let him go ever again. I couldn't think of anything else but my baby from that moment on. It was like when the judge hit that gavel, I released myself from caring why he chose the ugly schoolteacher over me, the woman carrying his child.

I didn't speak to Mr. Camry much afterward, but it wasn't long before he requested DNA, and I said, "Let me know when and where. And, I ain't paying a dime." A few weeks later, he sent me the information. He had paid for it and set up an appointment. I showed up on time with a big attitude.

He was like, "Hi. Thank you for coming."

I looked at him and said with a smile on my face, "Don't talk to me."

The tech asked who was taking the test. My smart mouth quickly said, "I know he's my son, so I don't need a test."

The tech swabbed Mr. Camry and then asked him to hold the baby. My baby started nutting up quickly.

"He doesn't know him and won't sit still for him. I'll have to hold him," I told her.

> Now I have no reason to come with a whole attitude. Remember I told another guy he was the father. Now that this man wants to confirm that this child was his, I shouldn't have had a problem, but I did. See how I added more stress to my life?

We took the test; well, *they* took the test. The tech said it would be three to four weeks before the results returned. I asked her how would I know when the results would come out.

She politely said to me, "You won't. He will because you weren't tested. Therefore, you won't get the results. If you had been tested, you would get them in the mail."

My mouth hit the floor. So, he could say the results say anything. I left with an even bigger attitude and didn't say anything to Mr. Camry.

I put my baby in his car seat, and I drove off. Three weeks would pass, and I wouldn't take any calls from Mr. Camry, well, until I needed some pampers. I called him and said I needed some money. He wasn't giving me anything. He hadn't told his family he had another child. He told me he would give me some money once the results came back.

Lo and behold, the next day, I would get a call that the results were in. He said, "I'll meet you and give you some money."

"Oh, now you want to give me some money. Why now?"

"The results came back."

"Oh really? And what did your schoolteacher say the results were, honey?"

"Why are you asking about her?"

"Because I know she's the one who read them first."

"Well, she did, but she won't have anything to do with this. It's between us."

"I don't think your country wife knows that."

We began to meet up in public places, then he would come over to my place to drop off money and see our son. It was usually after work, but he would come. I'm not sure why, but we didn't really have any big confrontations after that. His wife would continue to call, and she and I would continue to get into it. She would check his phone bill, get my number, and call.

I remember one time, after I had just moved and got a new house number and called him on his cell phone. The next day, she called and pretended to ask for someone else. I was like, "Honey, your husband isn't here."

She tried to play it off. "Our kids are brother and sister, and I would love it if they could play together." Her insecurities were really bad. I understood now why she was so insecure. But her insecurities had nothing to do with me. Still, she and I continued to fight throughout the years.

One time she threatened to jump me with her sister. Yes, this was all over a man. Now I wasn't innocent. I played my part in it. I was that chick, my mouth was really slick, and I had no filter. Thank God for growth and filters now because I was horrible with that tongue.

CHAPTER 8

In Love with Lust

After my drop-the-baby-off-on-the-doorstep routine, I considered allowing Mr. Bus Driver to start to come around me with my son. But I wasn't quite ready. I wasn't too sure about Mr. Bus Driver, so I never called him. It was time I moved from Decatur.

I made my way back to the South Side of the A, into Clayton County, Georgia. I moved into this co-op complex. Two of my good friends lived there, and they had two more of their high school friends who also stayed there. Wouldn't you know it was five of us single mothers living in this same complex?

We would hang out together, and the kids would hang out. It was a nice setup. If one needed a babysitter to go on a date, we would drop the kids off with one of the others. We went out most times together. We were the original Single Mom's Club. Haha!

I remember one weekend, in particular, when I thought I saw Mr. Bus Driver, but it wasn't him. This guy reminded me of him so much that I contacted Mr. Bus Driver and asked him to stop by. Little did I know Mr. Bus Driver had brought a house just a few miles away. Neither of us realized we were that close in proximity to each other. He was a ten-minute drive.

Needless to say, he and I started to hang out again. Nope, no sex was involved. He did show me where he had filed for divorce, but the filing wasn't enough for me. I wanted the actual divorce decree in my hands before I spread my legs again.

Mr. Bus Driver came over more and more as the months went by and, in that time, would see my kid and quickly began to form a relationship with him. My baby was a little over a year old, newly walking and running and getting into everything.

By this time, Mr. Bus Driver showed me the court date for his divorce. He had really started to wine and dine me. Still, no sex was involved until the day I would say was created by God. But since people got hurt feelings, I won't put that on God.

Mr. Bus Driver left my place and headed home. I thought he was gone for the night, especially since he had been there when my baby woke up, and he put my baby to bed for the night after he bathed him. So, this was an all-day-together thing. Well, he left and came back about thirty minutes later. At this time, I opened the door, and the look on his face was troubling. He rushed right in.

I was like, "Okay, calm down, hold on. Let me go get you some water. Drink the water, honey. What happened?"

He drank the water and then said, "Everything is gone. Everything."

"Huh? What are you talking about?"

She took everything.

"Okay, which she are we referring to, honey?"

He said GG, his wife.

"Oh." I laughed—well, on the inside, that is.

He was too upset to talk, and I wasn't going to push it. Now I was low-key excited because to me, in my head, this meant she was out the door, and now I could have him to myself. Poor little tink-tink was I cuckoo for cocoa puffs about this man. He was feeling so bad, and I was enjoying the moment.

I held him tight, and he started rubbing me. I started to rub him, and our hands just kind of did their own thing. But of course, one thing led straight into another. Before I knew it, I was com-

In Love with Lust

forting him with my legs wide open. I was enjoying every moment too, because, for some odd reason, I believed I had won. Imagine that, imagine me thinking I had successfully gotten this man to leave his wife for me. He was now officially mine.

No, the divorce wasn't final, but she had moved out of the house, leaving him with nothing. She left his clothes, an empty house and a lot of bills. The next day, he would wake up next to me as my baby came into my room from his.

Mr. Bus Driver rolled over and called out, "Buddy, hey, buddy," as he would call my baby. And my baby called him buddy. My baby just smiled, ran to him and jumped up in the bed. Luckily we were dressed. But he was supposed to be gone before my baby got up. At least that's what I thought should have happened. I really thought he stayed longer so my baby could see him. I told myself, *Oh well, I'm caught now. My baby ain't going back to sleep.*

We had breakfast, and then he left to check out his house and file a report with the police. He later asked us to come to his house where his wife had just stolen everything not nailed down. I reluctantly went. I wanted to see for my own eyes that this was real. I got there and saw everything was gone, just like he said. He was sad, while I was happy—well, on the inside. Soon after that Mr. Bus Driver and I started to experience life together.

About that time, he had an accident while driving the bus. Although the accident wasn't his fault, he couldn't pass the drug test immediately after the accident and they placed him on leave until the investigations had been completed. Meanwhile, I was looking for a job and a daycare.

Sista E

I remember one time I had a job interview but didn't have a babysitter at the time. Mr. Bus Driver said he would watch my baby.

"Huh? Are you sure?"

"Yes. I don't have much to do today, and he can come to hang with me."

> We womenfolk fall so in love so quickly that we trust this man with our lives and our children. We only see what we wanna see and think he's feeling the same way.

I returned home following the interview, and they weren't at my place. I called Mr. Bus Driver, and he said they were on their way from his parents' house in Decatur. I was in shock. *Why did he take my baby to his parents' house?*

I didn't ask many questions except for how was y'all's day, and he talked as I checked my child over to make sure he was in one piece. Hey, that was the first time in my child's life that he had been with someone who wasn't family. I was nervous all day, planning and plotting what I would do if my baby had one piece of hair outta place.

Mr. Bus Driver was passing the test on every level. He was around more, he was loving on my baby, and he was loving on me.

I once asked my dad, "How do you know if a man really loves you or not?"

He said, "It's in his actions. Men are not about words. But it will show in his actions. What he does for you, what he sacrifices for you."

Mr. Bus Driver had started fixing things in my place; he was even helping me pay a bill or two. It was now the summer. He and I were both looking for jobs. I worked on his resume and helped him with his job search. I figured if I keep him employed, he'll keep taking care of me.

My baby had been in Milwaukee with my parents for a few weeks and was ready to come home earlier than planned. I couldn't take his crying every time he heard my voice, so I went and got him. I had to take a road trip. It was also time for my goddaughter to go off to college at Tennessee State University in Nashville. My baby was in Wisconsin. I thought to myself, why not do a two-for-one roundtrip? So, I asked my boo, Mr. Bus Driver, to take a turn-around trip with me, leaving Georgia, stopping in Nashville, then running down to Wisconsin, and all in forty-eight hours. Needless to say, we had a nice little road trip.

He did most of the driving, and we laughed and talked and shared so much. He talked about his upbringing, and I talked about mine. We were bonding and connecting on levels I had never connected with any other man before. I loved every minute of it.

Everything was going great. Well, that was until I asked for that divorce decree again. Once we returned home, as I was lying in my bed after just getting done spreading my eagle across the land, I asked the infamous question, "What are we doing? Where is this headed? When will the divorce be final?"

"She keeps contesting the divorce. But our next court date, which should be our final court date, is next week. I promise, baby, I'll bring it over as soon as it's done."

Now in my day job, I was a paralegal by trade. I trust but verify for a living. I was definitely verifying what he was telling me.

Sista E

Now keep in mind I had asked him three questions, but he honed in on only one. He had sweet-talked me until I forgot I had asked two other questions—two important questions. What did I do? I rolled over and rewarded him with a ride on top of the mountain. Yup, more sex! We had sex so much that you would have thought we were honeymooners or porn stars.

He left the next morning, and that's when I realized he still didn't answer my questions. I thought, well, since technically he is still married and he didn't say we were in a relationship, let me keep my options open.

> How many of us women have been in a whole relationship with a man, but he wasn't in a relationship with us? We've committed and have been faithful, and he's still sowing his royal oats.

Summer was coming to an end, and I was still looking for a job. Now my bills were piling up, and my money was running short. Mr. Bus Driver was still on leave with the bus company, which would soon become his former job. And his bills were piling up too. We both had minimal income and major bills. I was about to be evicted from my co-op. He had a whole empty house, and the mortgage was getting behind.

As the weeks flew by, I didn't really put too much effort into Mr. Bus Driver. I had started to pull back from him—you know, keeping my options open. I started dating, nothing serious because I wouldn't have sex with anyone else. I would see Jimmy and hang out.

In Love with Lust

Mr. Bus Driver asked me where I was once, and I told him I was out with Jimmy. Mr. Bus Driver expressed his severe dislike that I spent so much time with Jimmy. I hit him with the "You're still married, so don't speak on who I spend my time with."

It was now Labor Day weekend, and this was our first big fight. He was upset and went and hung with his friends in Bankhead, drinking and partying like rock stars, while I was hanging with my girls. We had kids, so we turned Taz's place into the party spot. The kids partied upstairs, and the grown folks partied downstairs—food, music, and yup, you guessed it, alcohol, lots and lots of alcohol.

As the night wore down, Mr. Bus Driver popped up at my place. I wasn't home, but he could see the lights and music across the parking lot where my homegirl lived, and he came across and asked someone to go get me. I came outside and saw that it was him on his motorcycle.

It's the motorcycle for me. It wasn't him; it was him on the motorcycle. This man was looking so good. Picture this dark chocolate, standing six foot four and about two hundred sixty-four pounds of pure muscle, feet a size fourteen. Need I say more?

He was standing there looking pitiful, head hanging down, motorcycle gloves in his hand while hitting them together. I looked at him with so much dust and so much love in my eyes. He was so adorably cute. Naw, he wasn't cute. He was too much of a man to be cute. But *he sure is fine and mine* was the only thought in my head at that moment.

But I, Ms. Independent, had to play it cool as I walked out to him. "Yes?"

"I'm sorry."

"Sorry for what?"

"I don't want to fight with you anymore. Can I just hold you?"

In the back of my mind, I was like, *hell yeah. With yo fine self, you can have your way with me.* but out loud, I said, "Hold on, let me get Buddy straight."

Buddy was now two years old. I asked Taz to keep him because the kids had fallen asleep from their partying, then I came out and quickly jumped on the back of that bike.

> Let me see if I can explain the sensible intimate feeling of a bike ride. First of all, you don't ride with everyone. Nope, no way, no how. Everyone can't be trusted with your life in their hands like that. But for a woman to be on the back of your bike, holding onto you for dear life, that's trust. Holding onto you while you're in full control of the bike and her life, that's protection. What do most women want but didn't get from our fathers that we want and need in our men? Love, security, and protection. Add the wind blowing in your hair, and it's nothing but pure intimacy 101, the foreplay before we play.

We rode back to his house, just him and me. He offered me a drink. I had already been drinking a lot at Taz's place, but since he offered, I didn't dare turn it down. He put on some music, and we created our own little party.

He said, "I'll be right back. I'm going to the garage."

The mood was set in the house, and when he was taking too long in the garage, I went out to check on him, and what did I see? Him sitting there, smoking a joint.

I said, "You keep me waiting for you while you smoke?" I had no clue before then that he even smoked anything. He never smelled like smoke before. But it turned out he did, just not in his house or cars.

He asked me to join him. What did I do? Yup, you guessed, I joined him. Keep in mind that I hadn't smoked a joint since the early days of college. It had been about eight to nine years before this that I had ever smoked anything. I wasn't a smoker. But this night, I had a joint and liquor. I was just a regular ole party gal.

He blew the smoke from his mouth into mine, and that made it worse. I was severely intoxicated. He was in the right mood. I was in a darn good mood myself.

We took that party from the garage to the bedroom. Well, we tried to make it completely to the bedroom but took a few breaks to get there. He kissed me all down my neck to my chest down my body. I forgot where I was. We finally made it to the bedroom for the final showdown. And right before his grand ending, I had to get mine. I flipped him over and rode the horsemen until the sun came out. Well, the sun didn't quite come out. He flipped me over and did his best until I slipped and landed upside down, hanging off the bed. My head and back were on the ground, and my legs and feet were on the bed with this man. Needless to say, we both passed out until the sun came out.

The next morning, he complimented the late-night super-early morning activities and then said, "Move in with me."

"Excuse me?"

"I want you and Buddy to move in with me. Your income and my income and one household." I had just gotten the job I had interviewed for when he kept my baby for the first time.

> *There are two times you should think twice before answering a man's question. The first is when y'all are having sex, and the other is when he's down to nothing. Neither time is he thinking in full capacity, and sometimes—okay, most times—he's just thinking of himself.*

Now, I'm thinking, wow, he must really love me and want to be with me. I was thrilled, then I looked sad and said, "I can't move us into another woman's house with her husband."

He pulled out the deed that proved it was his house alone with a divorce decree. He said, "It's my house, and I'm a single man. Now when are you moving in?"

Yup, egg on my face. With tears in my eyes, I opened my legs real fast and gave him my answer as I was riding high on this horseman, thinking in my mind that I had finally won.

Now, remember, I was living in a co-op with my Single Moms Club friends. We helped each other out, whether it was food or babysitting or just like-minded folks. We were each other's support system, raising boys with no fathers.

I came home and told the girls I was leaving the safety of our compound. Needless to say, they didn't agree with me. But at this point, I had won. I was in love, and there was nothing no one could tell me.

He and I packed up my place and moved into his house. We even took the refrigerator. Remember, everything in his house that wasn't nailed down left with the ex-wife. The stove was nailed down. The refrigerator and the washer and dryer weren't. But I had a washer and dryer, and the co-op I was in had a refrigerator, and he said we needed it. So, we took it, and I helped him take it. And I knew it was wrong and would be charged for it.

I moved myself and my baby into this woman's house. Yes, technically, the house really was his, but it was the point that she called it home first.

I thought he and I were about to start our lives together, and everything he said was gold. So here I was, floating around like I got platinum pussy, like I was now queen bee.

> Why do we think we have to hurt another woman for us to feel like we're on the come-up? We get so upset and argue. We cuss and fuss with another woman over a man. And why? Ladies, here's a clue. If he doesn't shut the other woman down himself, if he doesn't put his foot down and explain to her and everybody else listening, this is my wife or my woman, and you will respect her as such, guess what? Then it means he can't shut her down because clearly, she is a factor. Then that means you need to be a

Sista E

> nonfactor and let them go, and you go in peace.
>
> I promise what God has for me is for me. I wrote that so you can say it out loud to your dang-on self. It just appears there are not enough men for everyone to get one. Well, there is. There are enough men for us to get one. The one for you will love, honor, and cherish you. He won't play games and will shut other women down just for you. Believe that in your heart, Sis.

It was September. We were a few weeks past Labor Day weekend and its festivities. My son and I had moved in with Mr. Bus Driver, and I had started a new job. Things were going great. He and I were getting it in as if we were rabbits on a honeymoon. My baby was still a baby, so he took naps often, and I took Mr. Bus Driver whenever I wanted to and as much as I wanted to. Hell, we were living together.

I thought life would change when you got married or settled down. But not Mr. Bus Driver. He didn't smother me, and he didn't question my goings and comings. I still had my freedom, my life outside of him, and he still had his. Things were going great.

I was invited to a college classmate's cookout, and I brought Mr. Bus Driver along. We walked in, and the crowd was jumpin'—folks eating, drinking, and playing cards. There were girls in the kitchen and living room, guys on the deck, shooting dice and playing cards. It was a grown-folk party. And, of course, I knew quite a few folks there. A couple of the guys spoke and hugged me. Mr. Bus Driver was cool and casual. He even went out back to play cards with the other fellas. I fixed him a plate of food and took it to him, and went on about my business. It was perfect, I tell you.

Well, on our way home, he was talking to me about the cookout, and he'd noticed a guy was interested in me and casually asked me about him. I explained he was a friend, a guy who was once interested.

He was like, "Yeah, he still is interested." But he was cool about it. He also said, "I see you're still pretty popular everywhere we go."

"It just appears that way. I truly am a nobody."

"Everywhere we go, someone knows you, and I'm the one who's from here."

"I went to college here, and I've worked here. Plus, I'm in a few world-known organizations."

I thought that was cute of him to act like he was jealous. I laughed, but in the back of my mind, I was like, *whoa, brotherman is paying attention. Let me step up my game.*

The medical insurance had kicked in with my new job after the first thirty days. Having been without insurance for several months, I set up an appointment for a physical. Nothing of alarm. I just needed to make sure my goods were good. You know what I mean?

I found this nice doctor named Barbara Washington. She was young, Black, and talented. She was gorgeous and sassy and feisty. I loved it because that meant we had a lot in common; therefore, she would understand me. She asked the standard question, "When was your last menstrual cycle?"

I pulled out my book again. "I'm not sure, maybe August, because my cycles aren't regular."

"Hmm. You should have had one by now, though."

"No, Doctor, my cycles aren't on a regular schedule. It comes when it wants to."

"Well, we need to find out why it does that, but for now, I just wanna run a few tests just to be on the safe side."

"Doctor, if you're about to run a pregnancy test, you'd be wasting your time."

"Oh really? Okay, well, here are these pills that will make your period start. I want you to take these but only after I call you back. Remember, now don't take them until after you get the call from my office. I just want to run a few tests and get the lab results to be sure and know where we are."

"Okay. You're the professional. It's just my body, and I told you I'm not pregnant."

"Well, I ran more than just a pregnancy test. As I said before, we're going to get to the bottom of why your cycles aren't coming regularly."

I picked up my now two-year-old, and we went home. Mr. Bus Driver was home, and he had cooked dinner. He asked what took me so long to get home. I told him it was traffic when I left the doctor's office.

"Oh yeah? What happened at the doctor's office?"

I was getting my baby ready for dinner and talking at the same time, so I couldn't see Mr. Bus Driver's face when I said, "It was a standard visit, nothing major."

"Okay. Well, dinner is ready."

Mr. Bus Driver was just as quiet as a church mouse during dinner. I noticed it but said nothing or thought nothing of it. However, the next day, Mr. Bus Driver said, "Are you sure you don't have anything to tell me?"

I was confused. "What are you talking about?" I was now getting an attitude because something had been off with him since I got home the day before.

"I feel like you're hiding something from me."

"I'm hiding how fat I am. Now leave me alone. I'm not hiding anything else."

He left home after that and went to Bankhead to hang out with his crew. I went on with my day. I got my baby ready to stay at his auntie's house for a few days as I would be in Philadelphia for training the following week.

Tuesday came, and I got up, got dressed, kissed him, and said, "We'll see you on Thursday." I went over everything because I was going to need him to pick me up from the airport when I returned. I gave him a kiss on the cheek and left. I dropped my baby off and got on the plane. I arrived in the City of Brotherly Love and having never been there, I, of course, wanted to sightsee. So, following my first day of training, I went sightseeing before checking into my hotel. I was relaxing, getting some me time—no man, no baby, just me and my peace. Afterward, I checked into my hotel and got situated, then called to check on my baby. All was well.

I took a shower because tomorrow would be a long day, then called Mr. Bus Driver. Now keep in mind, cell phones weren't readily available to everyone. I didn't have a cell phone, so I had to make these calls once I got into my hotel room. Anyway, I called him, and he had a whole attitude. He was upset. I apologized and explained my day because I thought he was upset because I didn't call him right away and let him know I made it alright and safely. Nope, this man began to tell me how he'd been waiting on me all day to call, and he didn't have any way to reach me.

"Well, I'm here now. What's all this for? Why are you tripping so hard? We don't get down like this."

He said in a very loud tone, "Your doctor called!"

"Okay, it's no big deal. She probably just wants me to take those pills she gave me."

Mr. Bus Driver became even more irritated that I was so calm about the doctor calling.

I knew it wasn't a big deal, and I couldn't understand why he was freaking out. I said, "Okay, I'll call her tomorrow before I get on the plane."

"Make sure you do. I'll just see you tomorrow, but call me after you talk to the doctor."

> You would think I would have been concerned that a man was worried about my health. Wouldn't you have been? Something should have crossed my mind like he's a little too concerned, like maybe he's given me an STD, or maybe he had an STD and wanted to see if I had one too. Nope, none of that crossed my mind. Instead, my silly little self thought, Oh, how cute. He must really love me to be this concerned about my health. Go ahead, get your laugh on. You

> were once silly about a boy too. I know it sounds ridiculous the more I type it. But I was in love, and you know how we act when we're in love. That man can do no wrong. He just loves me so much! Keep laughing. It gets greater later.

It was too late for me to call my doctor, so I woke up the next morning and went to my training class, and right before I checked out of my hotel, I called my doctor.

"Hello, Barbara, this is Shirley..." I'm laughing out loud here. If you remember those two names together, then you're telling your age.

I called and spoke with Doctor Washington. The nurse didn't say, "I'll take a message and have her call you back." And the nurse didn't say, "The doctor said..." No, the nurse said, "And your name is...?"

"Emori."

Before I could get my last name out, she said, "Oh yes, the doctor has been waiting on your call. One moment please."

Now my heart was jumping out of my chest. What's wrong with me? All the thoughts of horrible news were floating through my mind for all of sixty seconds before she came on the line. "Ms. Emori, how are you doing?"

"Well, I was doing fine a moment ago. Are you calling to tell me to start those pills?"

"Yes, but not the pills you think. I called you in prescription, and I want you to take them when you return home."

Doctor pills? Oh, Lawd. What's wrong with me? "Do I have cancer, chlamydia, or herpes?"

"Oh God, no, honey, you're just pregnant like I thought you might be."

"Huh? What? Well, Doctor, it would have been easier to swallow if you said I had one of those."

She laughed so hard. "Emori, wait, are you not happy?"

"Uhm, Doc, I'm clueless. You're just telling me this, but no, this isn't happy news. I'm not married, and this would be my second child with a second man. No, Doc, I'm not happy."

"Oh, that wasn't your husband who answered the phone when I called?"

"Huh? Oh no, he's not."

"Well, he was awfully concerned about your medical life."

"Really now?"

"I'll make you a follow-up appointment for next week. Know that you have options, and we can talk about those options next week."

I couldn't say anything for a few moments but finally got a "Thank you, Doctor Washington" out.

> Isn't it funny how if a man says three little words to a woman, a woman's whole 'tude changes? And at the same time, when a woman says three little words to a man, a man's whole 'tude changes. When a man says, I love you to a woman, she changes, and when a man hears, I am pregnant from a woman, he changes. He either becomes her

dream or nightmare just from three little words.

I called Mr. Bus Driver. I was out of time and needed to check out of the hotel and board the van to the airport, so my words were few. "I'm pregnant. Pick me up at four." I immediately hung up the phone, got in the van, and headed to the airport. But the look on my face didn't leave. I have always been told that my eyes talk, and they were definitely talking.

I was sure the van driver was flirting with me. He said, "What's wrong because you're too gorgeous to be this sad?"

"I'll be okay."

There was a gay man on the van, and he was like, "Whatever it is, God will work it out. You just trust him." And when I heard him say that, tears just started flowing from my eyes. I couldn't stop crying. Of course, these two males were freaking out.

I said loudly, "I'm pregnant!"

The gay guy was like, "Awe, that's so precious," and the van driver was like, "Oh," and immediately jumped out of the conversation. See? I told you when men hear those words.

Well, the gay guy came over and asked if he could touch my hand and said, "It just may be in God's plans for you. So please don't cry at the gift God has given you."

I wiped my eyes. I was no longer as sad. We reached the airport, and he hugged me. The van driver said, "Good luck."

I arrived home, and Mr. Bus Driver picked me up as promised. The ride home was quiet, just the radio playing and the whistle of the wind from outside. We picked up my baby and went home.

Mr. Bus Driver was excited to see my baby boy, and I was excited to see him as well. But the two of us didn't say anything to each other. In fact, I went to sleep in the room with my baby and not in the master bedroom as usual. I was still trying to process it myself, so I didn't have words for him. I couldn't tell you what he had going through his mind. I would sleep another night in the room with my baby. It was now Saturday. I was still processing that I was now pregnant with another man's child—two kids, two different daddies, and still not married. Not one positive thing came to my mind. I came out of the room and was cooking breakfast. I asked him if he wanted something to eat.

"That's all you have to say?"

I said do you want your eggs scrambled or fried?"

"Emori, are we not going to talk about this?"

"Honey, do you want toast with jelly not?"

He's now frustrated, but his cell phone rang, interrupting us. He took the call, went outside on the back patio and closed the door. He's now smiling and laughing with whoever was on that phone of his while I continued as I was. I fed my baby, washed and folded clothes, and watched TV. He came into the house after his very private call and went into the room, throwing clothes, hitting the wall, just making a scene. I turned the TV up louder.

He came out and stood in front of the TV. "So, when are we going to talk about this?"

I ignored him until I couldn't anymore. He picked a fight about the bathroom. "The bathroom? I'll clean it up once I finish the clothes and start to clean the house like I do every Saturday morning. But no, you want my attention. Now you got it. Why the hell do you have to go outside to talk? I guess she's making you smile. So, who was that?"

He ignored me, and I was then up and loud and fussing about nothing, still ignoring why he was really showing out. The next thing, he's looking for his keys.

"Oh, now you're leaving?" He still ignored me, so I stopped talking to him and went back to watching my TV show.

"Where are my keys?"

As I was folding clothes and didn't take my eyes off the TV, I said, "I don't know."

While still looking for his keys high and low, he was talking trash, mumbling to himself. I continued to ignore him and pretended to be laughing at the TV, when I was really laughing at his frustration.

About that time, he got mad enough that he walked out the door, saying, "You gonna hide my keys so I won't leave the house?" He grabbed his spare key and left, slamming doors and all. As soon as I heard the garage door open, I called out for my baby. He came running, and I asked him, "Baby, do you know where Buddy's keys are?" He ran off and went straight to where he put the keys and returned them. I fell out laughing so hard it was unbelievable. Keep in mind my baby was playing with his toys all while Mr. Bus Driver was in his feelings and looking for his keys. He knew his buddy liked playing with keys.

"So instead of you calming down and getting out of your feelings and asking everyone in the house, you just assumed I was trying to keep you from leaving. Nah, bruh, go on. Leave! See you later." I was so pissed he'd had a whole conversation with someone on the outside patio that I was having a whole conversation with myself. "You were laughing and smiling and all around in a good mood while talking to this person. I was looking and pretending not to be looking. But even you would have questions if the shoe was on the other foot."

So he was gone and upset because I wouldn't talk about what he wanted to talk about. And I was upset because he was talking to someone, smiling, and in secret. It had now become a whole thing.

Hours later, I assumed, after a few beers or so, he called me. "Hey, I'm just checking in to see what ya'll are doing."

With my 'tude still on, I said, "We're doing the same thing we were doing when you left in a hurry." As I was answering, I heard laughing and music and a woman! It was a female voice that had me perking up and listening to the background. I asked him with a full attitude, "Where the hell are you?"

"What's wrong with you?" Then I heard him say, "Aye aye, I want you to say hi to my baby."

"Your baby? What the hell?" I completely lost it. I snapped completely off. Then I heard him say to a female, "No, no, let me go so I can go see what's wrong with her." Oh, that brought out a beast of a whole 'nother color. Now I was a "her?"

A second later, I heard a female say, "Hello."

"Hello, who is this?"

"Well, who are you?"

Now, remember, it was him upset at me. He was the one who left and had taken a private call. I had remained calm the whole day. But hearing another female's voice and remembering that he had a private call on the patio before he left just set me off in one clean swoop.

I answered her question with full-blown 'tude, "Who am I, you ask? I'm the woman carrying his child. I'm the woman living in his house. I'm the woman who takes care of him daily, babe. Now, who are you?"

About that time, he had grabbed the phone from her, so it was him who replied, "That's my daughter." Then I heard him say, "Let me go. Let me go see what's wrong with her." Then the line disconnected.

I was heated to the tenth degree. Yes, I was 38 hot. I walked the floor the rest of the night. I put my baby to sleep in his bed. I had to pour myself something to drink to try to calm down, but it didn't work. Everything ran through my mind. He cheated with me while he was married. I was pregnant, and up until that day, he never had defined us. He never gave us a title. I was pregnant by a second man for the second time. All of this was running through my mind. I couldn't calm down.

I turned all the lights out and sat on the couch. The TV was on with no sound. I was trying to clear the voices in my head telling me I was just a fool. He didn't love me. *He's making a fool of you.* You know the voices from your inner self that remind you of all the negative and tell you that you aren't good enough?

Now I doubted myself being able to carry this baby to term. I was told I would never be able to have a baby because of the types of surgeries and sickness I had as a newborn. But here I was, pregnant again. And with the reminder of me not being married and about to have two babies out of wedlock—*not one but two babies.*

When Mr. Bus Driver came home, he asked, "Why are you sitting here in the dark?"

Sista E

"Who was that? Is that the person who had you smiling on the patio?"

"Oh, now you're talking to me? I've been trying to talk with you since you got back."

"What is there to talk about?"

He yelled, "You having a baby is a lot to talk about!"

I looked straight ahead at the TV.

He then came and sat next to me. "Is this baby mine?"

I gave him with the look of death.

> Ladies, we have to check ourselves as well. Remember, he and I have been down this road before. I had told him my first kid was his and then had come back and corrected myself. So technically, I shouldn't have an attitude. But, of course, I immediately got a whole attitude.

"Where the hell else have I been? I'm always with you. I don't have time to see another man. I've been with you and only you since I moved back. You know my every move and where I am. And how I know you know my every move is because you pop up to my friend's place when you get ready. But because you need to hear me say it, let me say it. I'm pregnant with your child! This is your baby! You and I are having a baby! You are my baby daddy! Do you feel better now?" I had no sympathy for him. I was real and raw with it.

Now I should have been understanding. But I just couldn't access that part of my brain at that point. I was still stuck on who that woman was.

He said again, "That was my daughter like I said earlier."

I got even more upset. "You let me look like a fool in front of your daughter? I don't want to talk to you anymore. I'm going to bed. Good night."

"You're running as usual."

"No, I'm not talking as usual." I laid down in the master bedroom.

Now, if I was really that mad, why would I go lay in that bed where he would lie after he had been drinking? Exactly. We girls really know how to get their attention sometimes.

He soon came to bed and said, "Good night."

I said, "No, it's not good," then turned my back to him.

Ladies, that is a no-no. Never turn your back to that man after an argument.

He looked at me as I turned my back and shook his head, then turned his back to me. He expressed he didn't want to have another child, and I expressed I didn't want to have another child out of wedlock. I was silent for a long minute, barely breathing.

Then I turned over and hugged him. "I'm scared."

He turned to me, and it was no more talking for the rest of the night. It was a different conversation, a nonverbal one, one that we both enjoyed, one that had ended us up in the predicament we were in—legs swinging, bodies moving. Instead of verbally talking our issues out, we went straight to what we did best—have sex.

Now don't get me wrong, it was always great sex.

Fast forward a few months, and I was still pregnant and showing. My one brother, E, and my godbrother had decided to move to the A. They came over one Saturday, and we cooked out for them. Mr. Bus Driver was starting to get close to my family—well, my brother, anyway. They were outside in the garage talking men folk stuff. And Mr. Bus Driver felt comfortable enough to tell my brother how he always got something on the side. Yes, a trick on the side. He said that's how all men did it.

My brother said no, that's not how marriage went, and Mr. Bus Driver then asked, "So you've never cheated?"

"No, never."

Now, my brothers and I are close. I'll fight you about my brothers. They can do no wrong in my eyes.

And Mr. Bus Driver pretty much just admitted he was cheating on his sister. Only an insane man would admit that to his girl's brother. Dude, he clearly had a death wish.

My brother then started to show him in the Bible how his thinking was wrong. I didn't believe that man ever listened.

> We girls have to learn to listen. What that man tells you and his actions follows it. Believe it! This man told me he didn't want another kid. I chose to continue with him and have my baby. He had already made his decision to not be a father. And he told me his decision.

As time went on, I had doctor appointments. I became a high-risk pregnancy, and Mr. Bus Driver missed every appointment. Lucky for me my brothers were in town. They were the ones babysitting my big baby, and they were the ones taking me back and forth to my doctor appointments. They were the ones I talked to about what was going on with the pregnancy, not Mr. Bus Driver. His actions followed his words. He didn't want to be a father.

The honeymoon was over for us. Sex was less, and his absence was more, and all the while, I was living in his house. By this time, cell phones were common. I would call his phone and get no answer. He would call back sometimes and ask me what's up, but many times he didn't. I would ask for something I was craving.

I remember one night I called him, and he answered. I asked him to stop by the Waffle House on his way home and bring me a chicken patty melt. That's what this baby wanted. I couldn't go out because my big baby was asleep, and it was late, so late I fell asleep by the time Mr. Bus Driver came home.

He came in, and it woke me up. I said, "Hi. Where's my sandwich? It's like one in the morning."

"I forgot."

"I asked you for one thing, and you couldn't do that. I don't ask you for much, but when I do, you could at least do it." I was screaming and yelling all while getting dressed to go get it myself.

He said, "Stop, I'll go."

I cussed him out from the time I put on my shoes and walked out the door until the time I came back and finished my food. This was the start of the end. I asked him for one simple thing, and he showed so little care for me.

He slept on the couch that night and many more nights after that. The arguments kept coming, and they were getting louder and more frequent.

Mr. Bus Driver had started driving a short distance with a trucking company by the time I was seven months pregnant, and he would leave at night and sometimes stay out overnight. I thought, "Hmm, this would be a good time." Yes, so he left for work one night, and the next night I was gone. I had packed up. My son and I left, no card, no sign of nothing, just gone.

He returned home and tried calling me, just to find out my telephone number had been cut off. Yes, I even had the telephone number disconnected. I was done. I took my kid and left, one kid in my arms and the other in my belly. I took the clothes on my back and dipped.

I called him two days later after my homegirl told me he came over there, looking for me. He started dropping by my friends' places, asking where I had gone.

I explained to him how I was tired of arguing and needed a break from him and that I wouldn't be moving back in with him. "You're not supportive of my pregnancy, and I was tired and stressed."

"If that's how you feel, then go right ahead."

I stayed in Mississippi with my big sister for about a week. I needed a mental break. When I returned to Georgia, I didn't move in with him.

When I left Mr. Bus Driver, I didn't take any furniture, just clothes. My brother had just bought a house in Fayetteville,

In Love with Lust

Georgia. I had the in-law suite to myself. Just me and my babies. So, I went to Mr. Bus Driver's place to get my TV and washer and dryer. I paid for those.

He wouldn't let me in. He let me knock and knock. He had a female there—his high school friend. But if she was just a friend, why not let me in to get my stuff? Nope, he wanted to cause a scene. So, in good fashion, I caused a scene.

He called the police. I had my brother in the truck, and he was like, "Look, bro, I don't have no problems with you, but this my sister."

Mr. Bus Driver was like, "Take your little sister and go."

I said, "I ain't going nowhere, and I bet you ain't gone make me." Yes, I was a feisty one. I stood 5'4"ish, but you would have thought I had superpowers as much junk I talked. But I was pregnant, and he had another woman in my house, and I wanted to prove a point to her and him.

Then the police showed up. It was a White female and another man. The female officer came and talked to me and asked what was going on. I explained to her I wanted my TV and washer and dryer out of there. "But he got another woman in here and doesn't want to give me my stuff."

"Well, if he asked you to leave, you have to leave."

Why, oh why did she say that to me? I went off on this poor little lady. I said to her, "Oh, I guess White women's boyfriends don't dog them out, just us Black, girls, huh? I guess your man has never cheated on you before."

And she just looked at me.

I looked at her and said, "Oh, so you don't know if he has cheated?" I then walked away from her and went to where the

Sista E

other officer was located while he was talking to Mr. Bus Driver. Mr. Bus Driver was sitting on the edge of his truck—a truck I helped him pay off.

The officer said, "Can we agree? He said you can get your stuff, just not today."

I looked at this officer and turned and looked at Mr. Bus Driver, then mashed my finger into his head and said, "I ain't going nowhere until this bastard gives me my TV. I'll come back tomorrow for the rest."

Mr. Bus Driver asked the officer, "You aren't going to do anything? You aren't going to stop her? She just mashed me in my head."

He said, "Yeah, I'll go get her TV."

I waddled away with my hands on my hips. Yes, I was good and pregnant at this point and yelled in there and told the ole girl she could have his cheating ass. "I'm done with him. Enjoy. You'll be pregnant and cheated on soon enough."

I got my TV, and we left. I would occasionally talk to him, and we would see each other, but nothing too serious.

I became sick with my pregnancy and was at the doctor's office more than usual. The doctor decided it would be best to bring my baby a few weeks early, and we scheduled a date. My doctor was very passionate about me having my baby at this historical hospital that was made for Blacks back in the civil rights era.

Now, if I knew the date I had to check into the hospital, do you think I told him the date? Yes, I told him, but he was a no-show.

I called him once I was settled in and gave him the room number. They started to induce me to go to sleep. The party got started, and still no him.

On Tuesday, I was in full-blown labor. I had no time to worry about who was there and who wasn't. The pain was there, and it demanded my attention.

The anesthesiologist had come in, but he was either incompetent or just plain slow. It took him seven tries to get the epidural in my back. My mom was there and started to fuss, and he got loud with my momma. I was in pain but told him that's my momma, and you got one more time to yell at her, and we gonna have some problems in here.

Once he finally got it right, the nurses were fine, but a few of them almost killed me. One was about to give me the wrong medicine until the head nurse came in and caught her. Another almost let me fall because she didn't lock the bed but tried to get me out of the wheelchair and onto the bed.

A lot was going on, and still no Mr. Bus Driver. Then it was delivery time. My favorite doctor, Doctor Washington, came in while on her cell phone dressed as fly as all outdoors. You would have thought she was heading to the club afterward. She had on a cute little dress and some stilettos. She spoke to me and everyone in the room with me. She said, "This little one is in a hurry to get here, so let's get him here."

Yes, it was a boy! I wanted a girl so much. But I had learned at a second ultrasound a month earlier that it was a boy. I didn't tell Mr. Bus Driver because he wasn't around, so I kept that to myself. But still, I thought maybe he would take off work and come to see his child be born.

Doctor Washington was still on her phone. I didn't know that she was, and she was in between my legs and talking. She looked up at me and said something, then looked back down and said something else.

I asked, "Are you talking to me?"

"No, darling," and pointed to the earpiece she had in her ear.

"Well, I'll be. I'm in the middle of labor pains, my legs are wide open, and you're on the phone like it's just another day." Well, it was just another day for her.

That day the hospital was busy with moms having babies. One mom even had to catch her own baby. Yep, the babies were just popping out. Right after I delivered my baby, in walked this absolutely gorgeous man. He was a resident doctor. I was trying to close my legs and see him. It was the most hilarious thing. In the delivery room with me was my goddaughter, my mom, and my good friend, and all of them laughed so hard.

I birthed the most amazing little human being who turned out to be a superhuman baby. But never did Mr. Bus Driver show up for his son's birth.

The time came to check out the hospital and take this little bouncing baby boy home with me. This was my second son and his first son. I called him again but no answer. He knew where I was, and still no show, no answer.

Three days later, Mr. Bus Driver came see our baby. Yup, not until a whole three days after his son arrived in this world did, he finally meet him. He held my baby in his arms, and the look was indescribable. He got his son.

The next day, I had my sip and see to show off my baby boy. It wasn't long after then the flurries of having a newborn wore

In Love with Lust

off. I would slip into this deep postpartum depression. Here I was, not married with two babies, two boys by two different men, and neither was around.

I remember when my oldest, who was three at the time, saw me dealing with my infant son and came in, yelling, "Mommy doesn't love me anymore," and ran off.

Hello, I was already in a deep depression. I started crying uncontrollably.

I called Mr. Bus Driver, and he came right over. When he got there, he saw all three of us sitting there, crying. I didn't even remember opening the door; he just came right in. He grabbed the boys and told me to go take a walk outside. "Leave the babies with me, and go get some fresh air."

This was the second-best thing this man had done for me. The first was to give me my baby. But I let that postpartum take over my life. That was the start of my healing. That was also the start of Mr. Bus Driver and me again. I really think he thought the baby wasn't his, just like the before. I know it bothered him the first time, and he didn't want to be disappointed again. He had already accused me of the second baby being the first daddy's baby.

We never married, nor did his cheating ever stop. He was true to who he was—a cheater.

Remember, when I met him, he was married or got married right after. But his cheating was a way of life for him. Twenty-two years later, and he still cheats to this day. But he would always get caught. His MO was the same.

He'd call me, see where I was and what I was doing, and say, "I'm liable to be over that way."

> How many of us know when he calls to see where you are but never shows, he's making sure you aren't near where he is about to be to make sure his two worlds don't meet up? That's his version of checking in. Trust me, that's not a good thing.

I was happy and continued doing what I was doing. But then I would call him, and he wouldn't answer, sometimes for hours. And sometimes, he would come over afterward. I soon figured out his methods, his games.

He never changed, and I continued to forgive. I guess I never changed either. He would cheat, I would figure it out and call him on it, and spread my legs again. But here's the kicker.

I soon found out he was cheating with his ex-wife. Yup, they had hooked back up. The tables had turned. I was the woman, and she was the mistress. Isn't that funny? Well, it wasn't funny when I was crying my eyes out. You get what you give. I started this situation as the mistress cheating with someone else's man. He never changed who he was; he never stopped. He continued to be who he said he was. It was me who didn't believe him, and it was me who chose to overlook and constantly forgive. It was me who chose to keep accepting the low-grade treatment that persisted.

Mr. Bus Driver and I continued to deal with each other, but I never moved back into his place. We continued to have sex and be involved in each other's life. He always had my boys, both of them. For the following seven years, he claimed both of my boys as his. He treated both of them like royalty. It was me he continued to treat like crap.

We would do family events and family vacations. We had made a whole life together. He continued to have side chicks, but I was the main chick. Every night he came over to my place or me to his. He was all my kids knew and part of our little make-believe family.

I was an insecure woman. I allowed and accepted whatever he gave me, whatever money and whatever attention. Every time I got paid, whether taxes or paycheck, he got something. Sometimes it was dinner or cash in his hands. We had our little favorite all-you-can-eat restaurants, and I remember one time even buying his drawls and socks as if he was one of my kids.

This would continue for years with Mr. Bus Driver and me. I would always assume oh, he'll one day choose me. And still, we would go through our moments.

Oh, he's not answering for hours. Okay, let me investigate who is it this time. And in true fashion, I would find out which one it was and forgive him and flop my legs right back open. It had become so routine for us. He'd behave and be the family man for a little while, then off he went. It was like a bad habit for him—two months on, one off, three months on, two months off.

I remember having our son's third birthday party, and Mr. Bus Driver never showed up. I felt so bad and so low. He embarrassed me in front of my friends. We waited for him, making the kids wait before we cut the cake.

I would buy the birthday gifts and tell the boys they were from both of us. I loved giving my kids big birthday parties. It was my thing. Mr. Bus Driver rarely made it to either of my children's birthday parties. I could probably count on one hand how many parties he actually made it to. But birthday number three for our son was the final straw.

About that time, I was living with a friend of mine, not working, and my grandmother took ill. I told Mr. Bus Driver, "I'm going to St. Louis for a few weeks to be with my grandmother."

In his mind, he would have freedom and no responsibility to me or the boys. He could roam free. He was excited. I was calculated. I was fed up and over it.

Until then, it had become embedded in my head that I couldn't raise my boys to men without him. I wanted at least one of my kids to grow up with their father and mother together. So, I allowed him to take the best young years of my life. I went with the routine.

From the outside, we looked like a happy family. Behind closed doors, the sex was great, but the arguing persisted. Then after my baby boy turned three years old, a light bulb came on in my head. Maybe it was Tupac. I gotta get mine, you gotta get yours. Get yours. And I ran to St. Louis.

I hadn't lived in St. Louis since I was three years old. My mom moved my brother and me from St. Louis, Missouri, where we were born, to Milwaukee, Wisconsin. Most of my family on both sides lived in St. Louis. I needed my family. By this time, my mom was in St. Louis, taking care of my grandma. And my grandpa had just passed away. I just wanted to be with my momma. I had done played the fool one too many times.

So, I left "Hotlanta" for the Midwest. In my defense, it was summertime. I got to St. Louis and was in heaven. I had my parents on both sides, my mom and stepdad and my dad and stepmom. I had my grandma and a host of cousins. I even had two of my brothers there as well.

I quickly got a job. My kids had to eat. I also enrolled in school. The mortgage industry had a major crash, and my line of work as a mortgage loan processor was over. I needed to reinvent myself. I had gone to college for social work but came out doing mortgages. Yep, it was time for a change on all fronts.

I had not told Mr. Bus Driver any of my plans. He thought we were there just visiting. He would call, and we would talk, and he would talk to the kids. And I would call, and he wouldn't answer.

Well, by now, I knew what him not answering the phone meant. And it did not mean he was in bed asleep. Well, he may have been in bed but not asleep and likely not in his bed and definitely not alone.

As I was around family, I found my strength. I started what was considered a decent job and was enrolled in school to become a paralegal.

Summer would soon be over, and I was done with Mr. Bus Driver's games. There were one too many butt dials for me. I overheard him talking to some woman, and I listened for a moment or two, then hung up and called right back. He, of course, didn't answer. That was the final straw for me, again.

Once he was done wherever he was and whomever he was with, he tried calling me. Well, this time I didn't answer. Now usually, I would jump whenever he called. I would get so schoolgirl gitty. Not this time. He called back-to-back, and I continued not to answer for about a week. And get this, nor did I call him.

Then he started texting and asking how the boys were. So, the next time he called, I answered. Nope, I didn't speak to him. I let the boys speak to him, and then I would hang up. I would let the boys call him whenever they wanted or mentioned his name, but never did I get on the phone. This went on for about three weeks. It was getting closer to time for school to start. My oldest was now entering first grade.

Mr. Bus Driver sent a text saying we needed to get my oldest registered for school. He also said he had gone out and bought some school clothes and stuff. I still ignored him until he called, and I put the boys on, and while he was talking to the oldest, he said, "Okay, put your momma on the phone."

Now usually, when he said that, I would take the phone from the kids and hang up. But this time, I could hear the frustration in his voice. So, I got on the phone. He sounded a bit surprised.

He said, "Okay, you've had your fun. It's time to come home."

"Is it now?"

"Yes. When are you getting here? We've got to enroll the oldest in school."

"Oh, he's enrolled in school, and so is Baby Boy."

"Oh, okay, you got that handled from there."

"I'm also enrolled in school, and I have a job."

"Oh, that's good. Wait, you found a job?"

"Yes, I did."

"Oh, that's really good, Ms. E. Now, what day will you be back?"

"I'm not coming back."

"What do you mean you aren't coming back?"

"It's that simple. My kids are fine, and I'm happy. I'm at peace, and you're full of drama and tears."

He was now at the top of his lungs. "You can't take my boys away from me. You can't do this."

In Love with Lust

"No, I can, and I did. My name is on those birth certificates, not no one else. You choose not to commit to me or us. You continue to have other women. Well, go ahead, keep them because you have lost me."

I hung up the phone, and he didn't call back. I felt so good and liberated. I felt free. I even felt happy, if only for a moment.

I would go on and live in St. Louis for almost a year. I stayed and worked, and the kids were in school. Until one day, my baby boy started having these full breakdown sessions about his daddy. At three years old, kids have no sense of time or location. But his body felt something because he would just start crying and screaming out of nowhere. "I want my daddy. I want my daddy." I would let him call him, and he would call them. But the baby boy wanted his daddy.

After the tenth public breakdown, I called Mr. Bus Driver. By this time, he had his parents living with him in the house we once occupied. So, I was comfortable enough to let my baby go to Atlanta for a few weeks. I haven't a clue what I was thinking.

I took my three-year-old baby to Atlanta and left him with this man. Now I was the one calling and trying to talk to my baby. One time I heard Mr. Bus Driver and some woman's voice with my baby. I lost it. I lost every bit of sense imaginable.

St. Louis had just had a snowstorm, but I was too livid to think straight. I got in my car and grabbed my oldest. Now I was in a snowstorm, going to get my baby from this dude who's got my baby over at one of his chick's houses.

I didn't have enough money to make the trip, so I called Jimmy for some money and explained to him my problem. He tried to talk me out of it. I was determined to go get my baby.

Even my momma tried to talk me out of driving in the snowstorm through the icy mountains of Tennessee to get to Georgia to get my baby.

How many of you know God protects the fools too? Everyone saw trouble coming, but they couldn't stop me.

Jimmy said, "I'll give you money to get home if you get here."

My momma said, "I'll ride with you."

And God said, "Okay."

I got in my car, a small sports vehicle, and went driving in the snowstorm. We hadn't gotten out of St. Louis County before we started to slip and slide all over the highway. I'm guessing God knew I would end up in jail if I got to Atlanta.

After slipping and sliding on I-55, we turned around, and I cried like a baby. I acted a plum fool, cursing him about having my baby around one of his chicks. I cursed his momma out, and I cursed out anybody who had something to say about me not being happy about him having my kid around some woman. I tried to curse her out too.

I was the one who left Atlanta for St. Louis. I was the one who ended things with Mr. Bus Driver. We were not together in a relationship, and we were not married. But I acted like a whole donkey. I endangered my life and the lives of my kids and my mom.

I couldn't see straight, I couldn't think straight, and all I saw was red. The storm broke a few days later. It was the weekend I was off work. I quickly drove to get my child and returned to St. Louis. I didn't say a word to him when I got to Atlanta. I wouldn't talk to him about it. I just showed up at his door, grabbed my baby, and left. Mr. Bus Driver's face was filled with pain and hurt. I didn't care. I just wanted my baby.

We got back to St. Louis, and I refused to talk to him for weeks until he sent me a text, apologizing and asking if we could talk.

I talked to him, and he apologized for his part. I wouldn't say anything. I did let him start talking to the boys again. He would always end their calls with, "Give your momma a kiss for me." And the boys would always try to give me his kiss.

My baby boy said, "Momma, take this kiss from my daddy." He was on the phone, and he heard it too. We both just laughed. That broke the ice with us.

By the time January arrived and we were talking more and more. I was getting homesick and over St. Louis weather. He and I started to make plans. He said, "Let's work it out. I want y'all to come home."

As February rolled in, I started looking for jobs and apartments because his parents were now staying with him at the house. And you know you can't have two women in one house; it just won't work. Besides, his momma didn't really like me, although she respected me. She would always compliment how well-dressed my kids were. She said her other daughter-in-law would keep herself dressed well but kept her kids looking like bums. And that would irritate his mom, Ms. Angel. She always had two pictures up in her house of my kids, one of each of them. She treated my oldest like he was her grandson as well.

We moved back to Georgia in March. We had a Black president, and Atlanta was the Black Mega. "Who couldn't make it in Atlanta?" was my thought.

My granny wasn't too happy about my decision. But she was alive. It was as if she was dying when we first got there but was brought back to life and living after having a lot of babies around. I know we were there for a reason—us being there brought life and joy back into my granny.

She would play with my kids and fuss at me. She fussed about them not eating enough and told me I was bathing them too much. It was funny because I said they were stinky boys and needed to be clean, and she said their skin couldn't take all of that water twice a day every day.

I learned a lot from my granny the older I got. I told her that Mr. Bus Driver and I had decided to get married. We wanted to make things work between us and raise our babies together. She looked at me and, just as plain as day, said, "Baby, he not the one."

"Grandma!"

"I know, baby. I know you love him, but he's not your one. He might be cute, but that's all he is."

I was so heartbroken that my granny didn't like my dude, and still, I left anyway and went back to Atlanta. I got an apartment while he planned to stay living in his house with his parents. But it was all good. We were still a family. We did more together. He was working, I was working, and everything was good. Right? Wrong!

It wouldn't take long before he was back to his tricks. This time I was curious to know who this chick was who had my man's nose wide open. Who was this chick, and why was she so important to him that he was willing to risk me and risk losing his boys and having to pay child support?

Mr. Bus Driver had a problem with child support. He said it's like women winning the lottery when they get child support. I know, stupid thought, right? I said the same thing. This dude was crazy. Child support is for the child's well-keeping and upkeep. But back to the story.

I researched and found out who this woman was. I wanted to know why she existed in our lives. More importantly, why was she still there?

I knocked on her door—bold move. Yes, it was a very bold and stupid move. You don't know what's going to be behind that door. I didn't care. I just wanted answers.

She was cool about it. I asked her if she knew who I was. "Yes, I know you're Mr. Bus Driver's woman and that y'all share kids."

"Correction. Kid. But if you know who I am, why are you still here?"

"He and I are just friends. We went to high school together."

"Oh, okay, if y'all went to high school together a couple of decades ago, then that means you can back up out the picture."

"That's his choice."

"You're correct, but what I'm saying to you, woman to woman, is I need you to sit back and get out of my way."

She said with boldness, "I've told him he's wrong, but he chooses to continue to come back."

"Do you know why he chooses to come back?"

"No, I really don't know."

"Oh, it's simple. Because you require nothing of him, and I require everything. I require him to be a man, and I require him to take care of his responsibilities to those in our house and those outside of our house, meaning his two other kids." I continued to belittle her, and I told her she would never be me. "He comes to you because you allow and accept his BS and games. You allow him to escape his realities and be a deadbeat. Now, you have to look inside, and you have to figure out why you want someone else's man and can't get one of your own. I can't help you with that."

I went on to say to her, "Tonight was a courtesy call. The next time I come back, there won't be no courtesy but some headbanging." I then walked off, headed back to my Lexus, and drove home to where he was with our kids.

Yup, I went home feeling like I had won. I couldn't get him to stop seeing her, but maybe I could get her to stop seeing him.

How many of us know a man is going to do what a man wants to do, and if he wants to go, he's going to go?

> Mr. Bus Driver told my cousin's husband once, "Ms. E is a good woman, and I know she is, but she ain't gonna be done with me until I'm done with her." Yes, you read that correctly. This dude knew exactly what he was doing. He knew I loved him, he knew I wanted to be with him, and he knew I thought I needed him to raise my boys. He knew my weakness was him. I loved his looks, his personality, and his family vibes. And he knew I enjoyed sex with him. That's the one area where we never had a problem; we were definitely sexually compatible. It was his character and integrity that were the worst.

He didn't directly lie. He just omitted the truth and called it truthful. He loved both of my boys. He potty-trained my oldest and taught him to tie his shoes and how to ride a bike. How could I not love a man for loving my son, who I said was his but turned around and said it wasn't his and then got back with him?

I believe this was the second reason I stayed with him so long. The first was I was programmed to believe women couldn't raise boys to men. That's a myth.

> Now it's true that to be a man, you need to see a man. Momma, that simply means put him in some activities where he can be around a man that you are not sexually active with. But we'll discuss this in my Momma, May I book.

I tolerated Mr. Bus Driver longer than I needed to for all the wrong reasons. But he had moments where his actions showed he loved me or at the very least deeply cared.

I remember when we threw my little cousin Dimples her 30th birthday party. It was Mr. Bus Driver and me with several other couples, plus the kids. I lived in some apartment at the time and had invited everyone over to celebrate with her. Our granny had been sick, so my cell phone was always near me. We had grilled and drank and just had a ball. Everyone was coupled up. Mr. Bus Driver and I were all hugged up, holding hands and laughing. Then my phone rang. It was Donnie who is the brother of Jimmy.

He said, "We've been looking all over for you. We knew you two were still in touch with each other, but we didn't know how to reach you."

"Oh, okay, what's up."

He said, "Jimmy died." I dropped the phone.

I couldn't breathe, I couldn't talk. I was dizzy, and I couldn't see.

I heard everyone asking, "What happened? What's going on?" Then I heard my cousin ask, "Is it Grandma?"

Now in my mind, I was saying, no, it's not. But they couldn't hear me. My friend Benita picked up my phone and called the last incoming number back. Dimples was now screaming and crying. Now everyone looked at me. I slipped. Okay, I fell out. I passed out. Mr. Bus Driver picked me up and was now practically carrying me back to the apartment.

Benita made the call and asked what was going on. Donnie told her, and she then yelled to everyone, "It's not Grandma, it's not Grandma! It's Jimmy!" I could clearly hear the sound of relief.

Then I heard Mr. Bus Driver say, "You crying over a dude? This dude at that?" He was heartbroken that I was clearly distraught over hearing of Jimmy's passing. He's saying, "If I knew you were falling all out over him, I would have dropped you back on that ground." I still couldn't talk.

Meanwhile, Mr. Bus Driver is expressing himself out loud with everyone that I was falling out over another dude. Benita got me some water and put me on the bed. He came in later and told me everyone was gone, and he'd put the boys to bed. Then he sat down on the bed, and I just laid on him. He laid next to me and held me until I fell asleep. He was still tripping on me falling out over this man.

He said, "When I die, are you going to fall out over me?"

The first words I could say were, "Die, and let's find out."

We had sex after that conversation, and then I went to sleep with him next to me.

Mr. Bus Driver had a jealous streak in him. He would play hard, but it bothered him that I knew people—a lot of people, influential people. It bothered him that I was moving ahead in my career. I tried to get him to see when I do good in my career, it's for our family. It's not just for me. But he couldn't seem to turn the corner and believe that.

CHAPTER 9

When Loving You Is Hurting Me

What is it with us that rebellion comes naturally? When we're told not to do something, we automatically do just that.

I was once told not to use my left hand, and without thinking, I used my left hand while doing something, and I'm a right-handed person. So, it should have come naturally for me to use my right hand. But because my doctor told me not to use it, subconsciously, I used the one I was told not to use. We do our hearts like that. We fall in love with the bad boys or in lust with the bad boys. Yes, it's fun at first, and yes, the sex is great at first. But when he starts treating you like community property and sleeping with many other women, or he starts causing you to do things that are not in your character, then, Sis, you have got to let him go and catch you.

I'm sure you've heard the saying, "Boys will be boys." Yes, they will be, but we women have to woman up and love ourselves more than we love them or hate them. Because it's our life. Our light that must shine.

Fast forward to Christmas. Mr. Bus Driver and I were not really together, although we talked every day, saw each other multiple times a week, and had sex each time we saw each other. And unprotected sex at that. He came over without calling, and we were once again doing the family thing—school shopping for the boys, raising the boys, doing family trips and events. We were, for all intents and purposes, a family, yet not a couple.

In preparation for Christmas, we discussed what we would get the boys. I said, "Well, the big thing for them is a bike. I can get everything else but the bikes."

Christmas morning came, and keep in my mind our baby boy always rose early in the morning. I had been up all-night wrapping gifts. Just before daybreak, Mr. Bus Driver used his key—yep, you heard that correctly—his key to my house.

> If his name ain't on that lease or mortgage, please don't give him a key. Make that brother man ring the doorbell for entrance like every other guest because the dude truly is a guest.

I was in my bed sleeping. He came in quietly, bringing in the bikes for the boys, placing them next to the tree. Then he did what he usually did—come quietly into my bed. We slept, well, for a moment, before he was in between my legs doing his best. Then we heard the pitter-patter of moving feet. One or two seconds later, the little one came and jumped in bed with us. The other walked in, rubbing his eyes. The baby boy saw all the gifts and went and woke up the oldest.

They were six and nine at the time. The joy, the laughter, and the smiles all warmed my heart. I was thrilled. I was happy. I had my three fellas, and they each had a smile on their faces. I was at peace.

I began to make breakfast while they were playing with the toys and putting things together. Baby Boy just wanted to ride his bike, and we promised he could go out after breakfast. So, while they were all in the living room, I went into my bedroom to get dressed. That's when I heard something vibrating.

I looked and saw it was coming from Mr. Bus Driver's things. After checking, I discovered it was another phone he had in his coat jacket. I called the number back, and yup, it was little ole Ms. Friend.

I told her it's Christmas and he's here, so don't be expecting to see him no time soon. "He'll be here with his family, where he belongs, so you can stop calling. And in case you were wondering, I spent the morning sitting on his face. So, remember that the next time you kiss him."

I hung up on her and put his phone on the bed to let him know I saw his hidden phone, and he could see I dialed her number back. I then walked into the living room and reminded him that he promised my oldest they could watch the game together today. Then I returned to the kitchen and finished cooking. For some reason, I felt accomplished, like I had officially run her away.

The next few weeks were cool. He hadn't disappeared and was with us all the time. We were working together to raise our family. And then, out of the blue, the shoe dropped. Yup, he disappeared.

I called and called and called, and no answer, no return calls. Nothing! With each call I made, I became more and more frustrated until he called back. Well, his butt called back. I could hear him with her clear as day say, "She's calling you. Why aren't you answering?"

He said, "Don't worry about her. I'm here with you." She started to say something then, but he cut her off and said, "Do you want to answer her? I'll go to her. Or do you want me here because I'm not talking about her?"

Yup, I'm the "her" they were talking about. I was devastated. I listened and heard what I had already thought and believed. Now it was confirmed, no more speculating.

My fears were now in my face, and I was thinking, *whatcha gonna do now?* Nothing, right? Wrong!

I gathered those bikes and left my kids with my sister. He had a truck, and I had a small car. I threw the bikes in my car and drove to his brother's house, where I knew he was. He wasn't there when I got there. His truck was there; they had left.

I knocked on the door and rang the bell, acting a straight fool. I then remembered hearing him say to her, "Do you wanna eat?" By now, I had known this man for ten years. So, I knew what he ate and where he would go on different sides of town.

I went to the only buffet I knew where he would eat. I walked up in there, and what did I see? I saw him, his brother, and an ole girl.

If looks could kill, I would be dead. They looked like they had seen a ghost. His brother spoke first, "Hey, Ms. E."

Sista E

I said nothing, just glared. It was, of course, a public place, so I couldn't really cause a scene like I truly wanted to. But oh, was it on.

I sat down at the table. The four of us—yup, we all about to eat up in here. So, the brother walked off to go get more food. Talking to Mr. Bus Driver, I asked, "So this is what we doing now?"

"Ms. E, we're eating, and don't do it up in here."

I took a few deep breaths, trying not to hit level thousand. She began to say something, but I quickly cut her off. "If I, were you, I wouldn't say a thing." Damn shole wouldn't even breathe this away. She then walked off and I said, "Yeah, that's your best bet."

So now it was just him and me sitting at the table. I said, "You do this to our family and think things won't change?"

"I'm just out having lunch."

"No, honey, you're out having lunch with this bitch. Now I'm about to be that bitch."

He walked off like he was about to go get some more food. She came back and went and sat with the brother. I walked over as she was putting food in her mouth and asked, "So how does my pussy taste? Because you do know he was home with me last night."

She put her fork down as the brother spat out his drink, and Mr. Bus Driver walked over with his plate. I knocked the plate out of his hand. "Dude, did you think you were about to continue to eat with this bitch while I'm here? I know you're dumb, but I didn't think you were stupid too."

The brother said, "Welp, I think it's time I leave."

Mr. Bus Driver said, "Yeah, I'm leaving too."

I said, "Hey, let's all leave because your truck is waiting on all of us."

He looked terrified and said, what did you do to my truck?"

"Since I help pay that truck off, it's our truck, and I can do whatever I want to do to it since you're out here doing whoever you want to." Needless to say, they left there in a hurry.

I followed them for a while, and then I got tired and became more pissed. The difference this time was I had found a way to make myself happy whenever he would make me feel small or ugly or bad because he was out sleeping around. I started seeing other people too. The problem with men is they really can't take what they issue out. I knew I couldn't physically hurt him, so I started to seek revenge and started seeing other men. Saying our relationship was complicated was an understatement.

> Sis, if you have to list on Facebook you're "In a Complicated Relationship," then go ahead and put "Single and Crazy" because that's what it is. Call a spade a spade. Stop staying in complicated situations; life is too short for those kinds of entanglements. Get out and free yourself.

I wanted to get out of this complicated situation, but my head and heart would never match up at the same time. I would say I'm leaving, then keep holding on to hope at the same time. I would leave, thinking if I left, it would make Mr. Bus Driver come back. Yup, I know, crazy thinking for sure.

Then I began to redirect my feelings of hurt and disappointment. Every time Mr. Bus Driver would disappear and not answer his phone, I called a man who would answer my calls no matter when I called—Officer Chocolate.

Officer Chocolate and I had gone to college together. He was from Detroit, and he played football at Morris Brown. I had a huge crush on him in college but was never bold enough to really do anything about it. We ran into each other while registering our boys for rec football. He saw me and yelled my name. I turned around and was like, "Hey," shocked he even knew or remembered my name.

His oldest and my baby boy were the same age. They ended up on the same team. He and I went out on a few dates and ended up intertwined with each other. I explained to him my situation.

Now Officer Chocolate was six foot five, three-hundred-something pounds of muscle mania, dark chocolate with big feet and hands to match, and yes, you guessed it, a bald head with a big dick. There's something about tall, dark, and bald, hence the name of this book.

I slept with Officer Chocolate every time as revenge. Now don't get me wrong. In this case, big hands and big feet really rang true. Officer Chocolate rocked my world each and every time and always left me feeling like, "Mr. Bus Driver who?" Never once a dull moment with that man.

But it was just that moment in time when I was lonely and needed to feel. I needed to feel loved—hell, liked—by a man. I needed to be in somebody's arms. I just needed to be wanted by a man because the man I loved was holding somebody else. This would continue for months, heck, well into years.

The turning point was the accidental butt dial. How many of you know some butt dials are not accidents? And this time, I just wanted someone other than Mr. Bus Driver.

I was in one of my complicated moments and decided I wanted Mr. Bus Driver to hurt like I was hurting from all the pain he had caused me over the last decade. I wanted to see if he gave a damn about me or was it all about my kids.

Mr. Bus Driver had the boys at his house with him and his parents. I went out drinking, and to have a good time. Whenever I drank, I always had to follow it up with sex. It was like the two went hand and hand.

So, on my way home, I called Officer Chocolate and told him to meet me at my place. I also called Mr. Bus Driver to tell him I'd grab the kids tomorrow because I was drunk. He said, "Okay, call me when you get home, so I'll know you made it home safely."

I was like, "Yeah, okay."

Officer Chocolate arrived at the same time I did. I pulled in, jumped out of my car, and grabbed him and started kissing him as I was unlocking the door. With my phone in my hand and my purse on my arm, I was now kissing him on the wall by the front door. We're kissing, and it's getting to be some heavy kissing. Clothes were starting to come off as we took this party up the stairs to the bedroom while dropping clothes on the way to the room.

I got him to the bed and jumped on top of him, and now I was calling his name loudly, "Chocolate, Chocolate!" Okay, yes, I was being extra. But it was good at the same time.

Oh, did I forget to tell you I was still holding my phone in my hand? Yup, you guessed it. Who but who was still on the phone, listening to my background, hence the purpose for the extra? Yes,

I accidentally and intentionally stayed on the phone so Mr. Bus Driver could hear and get a taste of his own medicine.

But why he stayed on the phone was what I wondered. Then I got scared thinking he might decide to come over while Officer Chocolate was there. I thought, *yup, I better stop playing with fire before someone gets physically hurt.*

I hung up the phone and continued my mission. The next day, I called Mr. Bus Driver to drop my babies off to me and pretended like nothing had happened at all.

He behaved for a while after that episode. That's what they were—moments of good, moments of great, and moments of sadness. At some point, you have to admit that moments aren't what you need. You need love and respect.

We were on the crazy cycle. Being with this man was driving me crazy. I had lost myself while trying to love him. I started doing things that were out of my character. And when you start losing yourself and start doing things that are not of your character, then it is truly time to go. It is time to let it go. TP told us to let it go because it's another love TKO. Yup, it was a total knockout.

Months later, I had become so frustrated that I totally lost my mind.

> *Sis, we cannot get so caught up in a man that we forget we have kids to raise, kids who need us. He just isn't worth it.*

I had to learn to think of my kids when I got to level thirty-eight hot and seeing nothing but red in my eyes.

This chick would still be around. I had already knocked on her door, sat down at IHOP, and had coffee. I had already cursed her out, and she still stayed around. It wasn't her; it was him. He chose to be with her. He chose to leave me and the boys and drive to her. Those were all his choices, so why was I coming for her? I didn't sleep with her, I didn't have kids with her, and I didn't love her. It was all him.

I was home, literally waiting on Mr. Bus Driver all day because he said, "I'll be over there." So, we waited to go eat, waited at the house, and eventually, night came and still no show, no call. And when I called him, no answer.

My immediate thoughts were, *nobody puts Baby in a corner. Nobody makes me wait on them.*

I got my boys situated with a babysitter, and I drove to Southwest Atlanta, where this chick lived. And lo and behold, what did I see? A green truck sitting in her driveway. Yup, he was at her place while we, his family, waited for him.

Now, pay attention. It's going to go fast from here.

I blew my horn as loudly and as long as I could. I acted completely out of character. I got indignant for real. I set the neighborhood on fire—metaphorically.

I got out of my car and started beating on his truck. No response. I started beating on her car. No response. I got back in my car and laid on my horn. The neighbors started looking out. Oh, I was loud and indignant until finally, he came walking very fast toward me, saying something under his breath.

He reached into my window to grab me. He wasn't trying to hug me. And my reflex kicked in. I hit my window to roll it up, and I hit the gas pedal at the same time. It was as if it was one swift motion. Yup, he was caught up in my window by his elbow. He was hanging onto the car for dear life.

I was now driving, no, speeding down the street while he was hanging off the car. He was yelling something; I hadn't a clue what he was saying. All I knew was he reached in my window, and it wasn't for a hug.

Now I was going upwards of fifty miles per hour. I hit the brakes at the same time as I let the window down. Yup, you guessed it, he went flying. He landed on the sidewalk, but he was in one piece. Well, his feelings and manhood were shattered into pieces. But my face and neck were untouched because he didn't reach in that window to hug me.

I stayed in my car, antagonizing him for a bit longer. He walked back to his truck. I drove alongside him. At the same time, we were talking. Some might call it arguing. I called it "getting an understanding."

He had hurt me emotionally. I wasn't going to let him hurt me physically, and I had a whole big ole vehicle as a weapon.

No, sweetheart, that's not how the story goes.

He walked, and I drove back to his truck and his phone. He called the police. I sat there a bit longer, still antagonizing him a bit more. He had the look of disgust and hurt, and he looked as if he was in pain. I didn't care. It was either him or me, and it definitely wasn't going to be me.

I soon drove off laughing. But the police pulled up before I got far, and he told them to stop me. They came behind me and turned their lights and siren on.

I pulled over with a straight face. "Yes, Officer, how can I help you?"

He said, "I need you to come back."

I said, "Sure," just as sweet and calm as could be. Little did Mr. Bus Driver know, we were in Officer Chocolate's zone, and I had already called him while driving away, so he was on the phone as the officers pulled me over.

The officer on scene asked me what happened. "I don't know. He told me to bring our son's paperwork over for his signature, and I did, sir."

"He says you messed up his arm and dragged him."

"Sir, I'm five foot five. Does it look like I can drag that man anywhere?" *I said it with a straight face and with all sincerity in my voice.* Then to add insult to injury, I added, "I was gone when you all got here. There were no arguments, no problems at all."

The officer ran my plates and name and then said, "Ma'am, you have a good night. Go on home."

"Yes, sir." I drove off with a smile on my face.

Mr. Bus Driver was upset for about a week before he came crawling back on his hands and knees, and what did I do? Yup, I turned that booty up. I put it on him as if it was our honeymoon.

> How many of us know sex is not a healer?
> You can't keep masking the pain with sex.

Sex was the place we never had problems. He had turned me out to be just as freaky as he was. Teaching me how to please him in the different positions and places—yup, we had an awesome rhythm together. He was nine years older than me; therefore, he was a lot more experienced. But in my mind, I thought if I gave him the kind of sex he wanted, he would stay. I thought if I put my comfort aside, it would keep him. So, every time he came over, I was opening my legs or bending over for him. I thought doing this freaky sex and raw without a condom meant he loved me, and he would stay. Nope, it just meant I was the wet pussy for the day and sometimes for the moment. There were many times he left my bed to head to another's.

I cooked, I cleaned, I sucked, and I...well, you know the rest. But nothing kept him. I had his kid and hell, his boys, as he would tell the world. I gave him money and bought him things. He had my undivided attention much of the time. My focus was him and not me. Do you see the problem?

I poured into him what I should have poured into me, into my kids, and into my dreams.

As my brother once said, "You gave all the right stuff to the wrong man."

CHAPTER 10

Between You and Me

Do not continue to keep accepting less than you deserve. If you gotta force him to be with you, leave 'im. If he has to force himself to like or love you, leave 'im. If you have to force him to respect you, then leave 'im. Leave it. Just plain ole stop it! Seek peace and pursue it.

Sis, please know, you can't live in fear for what's around the corner. You have to remember action has consequences, good or bad.

Mr. Camry would see our son in public places because his wife, the schoolteacher and my boyfriend, Mr. Bus Driver, were both convinced Mr. Camry and I were still sleeping together. I knew it was my boyfriend's guilty conscience and the school teacher's insecure heart that they accused us regularly. Mr. Camry and I didn't argue; we didn't have many problems.

He saw his kid at parks or his job while I was picking up money. My son called Mr. Bus Driver Buddy. He wasn't his daddy, although he did the role of father. I wouldn't dare confuse my child and allow him to call another person his dad.

Mr. Camry knew I was with Mr. Bus Driver. The two even had an encounter or two—wait, maybe three. I knew Mr. Bus Driver was low-key jealous of Mr. Camry, but I didn't care. I knew the thought Mr. Bus Driver had in his mind about Mr. Camry was that this man had been with his woman because he messed up. And I knew it bothered him. But again, I didn't care. I figured if Mr. Bus Driver hadn't lied about being married, I wouldn't have met and slept with Mr. Camry. Yes, the plot thickens.

Over the years, Mr. Camry and I had become friends. The last drama we had was the DNA test, and even that wasn't big drama. It was me in my feelings. Mr. Camry would continue to see our son periodically. He didn't raise our son, but he contributed financially, and he saw him when we could. You see, Mr. Camry had built a life that he didn't like. He became a workaholic, and he poured himself into his work instead of being at home. He knew it was a mistake to marry the schoolteacher, but he ran scared. She had already had a kid, he had a few kids, and I had none. So, he felt she was more available and equipped to enter into a readymade family than I was.

In the long run, he and I weren't made for each other in any case. We tried to go back and reminisce, we tried to go back and see if things were a possibility, but it was just fun sex.

I remember one time after Mr. Camry had divorced the school teacher, he came to my job, but I cannot remember how I ended up on the office conference room table, and he ended up in between my legs. Yes, what a wonderful lunch break that was. We tried to rekindle what we had, but we could never find our grove. He was divorced, and I was on one of my many breaks from Mr. Bus Driver.

I distinctly remember sending Mr. Bus Driver to pick up my boys from the daycare while I was at home, playing with Mr.

Camry. I believe the sneaking off made it more interesting for us. We never went anywhere like on a date. It was just sex and conversation. But I couldn't connect to him, and that's maybe because he couldn't connect to our son. My oldest son, although he was biologically Mr. Camry's child, had more of a bond with Mr. Bus Driver.

I went to Mr. Camry's new apartment, and he had all of these pictures of all of his kids, but I didn't see a picture of our son. I thought that was strange. I went over to Mr. Camry's mother's house, and she had a wall of pictures of her sons and her grandchildren. It was like a trophy wall. But nowhere did I see a picture of my son. I truly felt some kind of way. I felt so bad that I would cut off playtime with Mr. Camry because I saw no pictures of my baby.

Still, we remained friends, and we remained close. We talked about some of the oddest things, but we still talked.

If you are truly friends, when the sex ends, you should still be able to be friends. Now don't get me wrong. It took life happening to cause Mr. Camry to grow up and me as well. We were better once we matured, although he was twelve years older than me. We both had to grow up and handle things a lot differently in our older age.

For twelve years, I would continue to go back and forth with Mr. Bus Driver. I loved him. I did, but was it deserving? Was it worth me losing me? The answer is no, it wasn't, but he was a lesson I had to grow through. And when I finally grew up, when I could take no more pain, no more tears, when someone finally gave me the mirror, and I saw me, and what I had become, I grew up.

I realized my pussy couldn't keep him. Me having his baby wouldn't keep him, and me buying him wouldn't keep him. I realized when a man wants to be kept, he'll stay. I wasn't what he wanted because if I was, he would have done what it took to keep me.

He figured I would stay a little girl and stay forever, or at least until he was an old man and tired of playing the field. I had wasted my good, young years on a man playing with me. He stole my youth, but I allowed him. He was a lesson learned even after dragging him with my car and him having permanent nerve damage from that incident.

We got back together even after all of the police calls. Even after everything, I continued to take him back. I loved that man to my soul—well, at least I thought I did.

I heard that line from a movie or TV show. *I loved him to my soul.* But the truth is, I was in lust. There is a major difference between love and lust.

I remember there was a time when Mr. One Time had called me well into the night, and Mr. Bus Driver got upset. He rolled over and went back to sleep. But it bothered him. The next morning, we were at full yelling status. We were fighting and arguing over other people when the truth was we had no business ever being together. I was the rebound girl from his ex-wife, and he was my rebound guy. And we all know you can't be with the rebound forever.

It wasn't until my baby cried, screaming, "Mommy and Daddy, stop it!" that I realized what I was doing to myself and my children. I saw my baby crying because he saw his parents fighting. I had to let go at this point. Things were just bad with us. Sex would become nonexistent, but the arguments were at an all-time high. We argued about anything and everything. We were arguing while I was at work and when I got home. It was everything and anything that caused us to argue. This went on for a year.

I had suspected he was over there with Ms. She's Just a Friend. I couldn't figure out why he chose her and not me. She wasn't better looking than me, she wasn't a better dresser than me, nor was she smarter than me. But she had no kids and no responsibilities. And with me, I had bills and babies, and I reminded him of how inadequate he was. And I was getting worse with the disrespect... He had made me an insecure woman. The only fight I had left in me was my words.

By this time, we were seeing each other less and less and talking even less than that. I had chosen not to have sex with him any longer. I would still get upset when he didn't call or show up for the boys. He wasn't trying to co-parent or come to any of their football games or school productions as he did when we were together. Every time I asked for money, his line was, "I only got $20."

At this point, I had become a drunk. I was stuck on my woo-woos. I was drinking when I made the boys breakfast. I was drinking all day. I was slipping into a deep depression. I was mean to my kids and family, and friends. I was hiding how depressed I really was. I was going through the motions.

> How many of you know, at some point, we all wake up sooner or later?

Sista E

It was football season. My baby boy was eight years old, and he came home from school with a stomachache on a Thursday. I did what we do—assumed he needed to go potty, go number two. I had him go sit on the potty for a while to see if that helped. Well, we went to bed, and he didn't mention his stomach again.

Friday came, he went to school, and by Friday night, he was running a fever. I gave him some Tylenol, put a cold towel on his head, and sent him to bed. I again assumed it was no big deal.

Saturday morning, my baby woke up with no fever and no stomachache. Great, all was well, just a little bug. Whatever it was, it was gone now, so let's go play some football.

His games were early in the morning about 10:00 a.m. He played the best game he had played all season long. I was so proud of him.

By the time we got to my oldest son's game, it was cloudy and starting to rain, which was around 2:00 p.m. A short while later, a friend of ours named Tony told me Baby Boy was up by the concession stand, sleeping, and I thought, oh, okay, well, he's probably tired. We had to get up early that morning, and it had been a long day. Plus, it's raining, and rain makes you sleepy.

My oldest was balling out of control at his game in the light rain. I didn't even go and check on my baby boy. I assumed all of the above but never went to confirm anything. We got ready to go, and I got to Baby Boy, and he was warm. I said, "Okay, let's get home, and let me get some food and fluids in you."

We got home. I fed him and gave him more medicine. He went to sleep. The night went on. I put ice on his head, trying to break that fever. But nope, that didn't work.

Between You and Me

About 3:00 a.m. Sunday morning, my baby came crying in my room. It was a different kind of cry. Plus, he was burning up to the touch. I woke up my oldest, got us dressed, and headed to Piedmont. I knew then something was wrong with my baby, and it was bigger than me.

They rushed my baby to the children's hospital, and by 6:00 p.m. that night, he was in emergency surgery, getting his appendix removed. Well, what was left from his ruptured appendix?

I was scared and felt all alone. I started calling Mr. Bus Driver at about 3:30 a.m. that morning and continued to call every thirty minutes, but no answer. I was sitting in the emergency room with just me and my babies, one scared and the other sick. I had no one to call on but God.

These doctors were moving like crazy, and I was getting more frightened by the second. About the time 8:00 a.m. arrived, I called his mother and briefly explained to her what was going on. I told her to call and get him here. He didn't show up until 6:00 p.m. that night.

Mr. Bus Driver came slow-walking as they are about to take our baby into surgery. If looks could kill, he would be dead. I gave him the death look. My baby was happy to see him as he was being rolled off. By that time, my family had gathered in the waiting room, and we prayed, and I cried. I couldn't sit down for anything.

They said it was supposed to be a simple surgery, in and out within one hour and in recovery for another hour. Nope, it was four hours.

He came rolling out, and we kissed him, and everybody left. My baby wasn't out ten minutes before Mr. Bus Driver was out the door. He left me and our sick son there.

He came back the next day for about thirty minutes. I asked him one question, and that sent him off. My baby boy would spend ten days in the hospital and three weeks sick, and we didn't see nor hear from Mr. Bus Driver again for months. But trust me, I knew after everything that had happened and everyone else showed they cared for my baby.

I grew up. I grew up, and I let go just like that. It was like a blink of an eye.

From that day to this, I refused to argue with him. I refused to wait on him to come to see my baby. I refused to ask for money or anything concerning my baby boy or the boys, period.

Once my baby boy was better and back in school, I immediately filed for child support. I always thought the moment you get the folks involved, it's no longer personal but now business. It was no longer about my feelings. It was strictly about supporting our son.

It was as if all the love dropped out of me. I no longer cared if he was coming over or if he would buy the boys something or if he talked to the boys. I was no longer afraid I couldn't raise my boys to men. I no longer cared where he was sticking that community dick. I simply wasn't checking for Mr. Bus Driver any longer.

After twelve years and a broken heart, I didn't care. There were no more accidental butt dial calls and no more calling from a blocked number to see if he would answer his phone. There was nothing left in me to give to him or that situation.

When I almost lost my baby boy, after him being in the hospital for ten days, after two emergency surgeries, him being sick for three long weeks altogether, something in me shifted. I couldn't muster up the strength to nurse my son back to life and run behind Mr. Bus Driver. I only had strength for my boys. All the love I thought I had for Mr. Bus Driver had disappeared.

> Isn't it funny how when something happens that's life or death, you forget all the pettiness, and it all becomes pointless?

> I found strength in me to go to church and truly seek God. I stopped drinking, I started reading my Bible, and I started living. I found a great job. It was as if a light bulb came on and everything started happening for me. I kicked into mommy mode, and I found myself.

Mr. Bus Driver noticed the change too. When he finally started calling, I allowed the boys to answer my phone. I no longer talked to him. Of course, he didn't like that, so he started poppin' up at my place. He thought he knew our schedule: work and school, then football practice, home for dinner, and then bed.

He came over to try to see my kids while I wasn't there. Yup, they became latchkey kids. But on this one day, the boys weren't home. The neighborhood kids told us a man stopped by and was asking questions about where we all were. I became infuriated, so I packed up and moved. I moved without his help or knowledge.

He no longer knew where we stayed, so he could no longer pop up at my place when he wanted to. I had had enough.

December came, and he was notified that he had an open child support case. Just to be vindictive, he requested a DNA test on our son, who looked just like him. We would hear every time we went around his people how much our son looked like him. But to piss me off and prolong the case, he requested DNA.

Our son was eight years old by this time. He was old enough to understand what was going on—well, partially. He could read the words "child support office." He questioned me why we were there. Mr. Bus Driver was good for involving the boys in what the adults had going on. He told the boys, my parents, and anyone who would listen that I tried to kill him when he got dragged.

I called him on our way to the child support office for the DNA test and put him on speakerphone. *Here, tell your son why he has to go to the child support office and take a DNA test.* But Mr. Bus Driver didn't answer his phone, so, I left a voicemail. "You need to explain to your son why you believe he isn't your son." Yup, I got messy and petty right along with him. But I was smart enough this time to take the DNA test with my son so I could get the results as well. This time I was certain who the father was. I had no doubts. But to have to tell our son why we were there was devastating.

Another win for Mr. Bus Driver, I thought to myself. But I didn't let that stop me or get me down. I continued to not talk to Mr. Bus Driver, and when he called, I put the boys on without me saying hi or anything. That continued until one day, I had to check him.

I said, "Look, this is the bed you made, now lay in it. Stop telling my boys you are going to see them, and stop asking them where we are. Stop trying to get information out of my kids. You can see them any time. Simply send me a text of the when and where. No, you will not come to my place to see them. And since I haven't a clue what's really going on in your world, you cannot take them with you. And the only place I will drop them off is in public or with your parents. But most importantly, stop telling them you're coming to see them."

It would be almost six months before he would call again. Of course, I wasn't calling him. I kept making excuses to my boys why he wasn't calling. I explained to my boys, "It is not your fault, and it wasn't anything you guys did. Buddy and I just weren't meant to be together, but he still loves you guys."

I remember we were at the laundromat having this conversation, and my oldest son said, "Yeah, well, if that's true, then why did he leave us? We were his boys."

My heart broke when my eleven-year-old baby was wise enough to see through the BS. I couldn't say anything but "I don't know." We have to consider all facts from a kid's point of view and then realize how our actions as adults are affecting our children.

Mr. Bus Driver and I would not get back together this time. This time it was over for good, and no looking back. When I closed my legs, he stopped being a dad. And that's not just how it appeared; that's exactly what he did. Then he went around to people who knew us and told them I turned his boys against him when in actuality, he turned the boys against him by not showing up and not keeping his word.

A few times, he met them at the park to play basketball. I would drop them off and then leave them for a few hours. But that didn't last long. He saw them that day after six months and said, "Wow, they are really growing up."

I was like, "What were they supposed to do? Stop growing because you aren't around? Our lives didn't stop because you stopped being part of them."

I had gotten to the point of no longer caring. I had no feelings toward him at all. I didn't love him, and I didn't hate him. I just didn't care any longer. He wasn't paying child support, and I had to remind the courts he wasn't paying even though it was court-ordered. He wasn't co-parenting. He wasn't buying clothes, food, or anything. He was giving nothing, and I had no emotions left to give him. It took me one full year to get over him totally.

The reality is some relationships come to an end—some abruptly, some over time, some never at all, and some come back together. But the truth is when you grow up, you realize it's you who you need to fall in love with first—well, right after God. But once you begin to love yourself, you'll never settle for less again. You'll never take mediocre again. You'll do things differently, and you'll learn from the hard lessons taught.

As we were told, experience is a good teacher. And in my experience, living this life to the fullest is better than crying through it.

Between You and Me

Make each moment count, Sis. You can't
live in fear for what's around the corner.
You've got to let him go and catch you!

CHAPTER 11

Clark Kent *is* Superman

When a superwoman needs her Superman to feel safe and comfortable and protected, it's not always about dick. Intimacy isn't about sex at all. But it is sexual.

Those of us who are known as the alpha females are always taken as strong, independent movers and shakers. We are always the dependable ones in the family, the ones who the world goes to when their world crumbles and falls.

The alpha female doesn't show weakness or fear. She grabs her balls and gets it done, no questions asked, no complaining, and most times without any help or minimal help from anyone.

The alpha female yells, "I am a woman! Hear me roar. I am me, and she is me." But never yells, "Help me!"

She smiles in the eyes of the public but cries in her pillow at night. Her family, friends, and faith always come before herself. She is an overachiever by day and a perfectionist all day. She is the alpha woman who says, "Watch me roar," then soars like an eagle in the sky.

She can think like a man, handle business like a man, have sex like a man, and fight cancer like a girl. We all know when a man gets sick, he becomes a baby. But when we get sick, we're thinking and strategizing on what's next. The alpha woman thinks and believes, "I don't have time to get sick and stop. We have no time to act like a baby. We have to boss up in all adversity."

But truth be told, sometimes we just need Superman's arms to hold us in the weariest of times. We don't want to tell him to hold us, and we don't want to ask him to hold us. We definitely don't want him to talk. Don't try to solve it all the time. We just want him to see that we've bossed up all week long, and now we just need his arms. No arguing, no sex, nothing. "Just kiss me on the forehead and pull me in tight."

I met Clark Kent and didn't realize he was my Superman. I didn't realize he was my Superman because he was not my normal. He wasn't what I was used to. He didn't have the swag like all the others. He wasn't loud and boisterous, arrogant, or cocky. He was a gentle giant, and I played him like a flute. I played Clark Kent like he was a poot butt simply because he wasn't dressed in the Jordans or Tims. He wasn't in the gray jogging pants. He didn't wear a uniform like so many of my men before him. He was a simple man.

He worked in the mailroom at my office. He wore glasses and smiled all the time. I didn't know what kind of car he drove because I only saw him driving the work vehicle. I didn't give him a second look.

He paid me so much attention that it turned me off. He knew my favorite color, and what kind of flowers I liked. He knew when I ate chocolate and why I was eating the chocolate. He paid attention to my every detail, almost like a stalker. But he wasn't stalking me. He was just paying attention to me—something I hadn't gotten from any other man before. Therefore, I wouldn't know what a man paying attention to me would look like. My own father couldn't tell me as much as Clark Kent knew about me.

He was the only one to bring me packages. Yes, others worked in the mailroom, but only *he* brought my mail to me. If I had a delivery of any sort, it would be him who delivered it.

One day I was overwhelmed. Work life was out of control, and so was home life. Clark Kent came into my office as my head was down on my desk. He knocked on the door and asked me if everything was all right.

I raised my head slowly and looked up with a smile. "Sure is. How are you today?"

He responded with, "I am blessed and highly favored."

Now I don't know if it was the stress that made me see him at that moment or if something was different about him. But when he said that, I actually took a look at this man as if seeing him for the very first time.

He had on a short-sleeve polo shirt, and he had arms. Arms for days, his muscles were just busting out from that shirt. Well, maybe not busting out, but it sure appeared that way in my mind. I looked again and saw his shoes—size fourteens staring me in the eyes. Then I saw the jawbone—just as firm and squared off as could be. Guess what else I saw, ladies?

> *Why is it we never notice the good guys until after Jody had us crying?*

There was no ring on his finger but a book in his hand. I asked him what the book was, and he told me.

"Oh, that's an awesome book." He smiled so big. Then I said, "Well, you'll enjoy reading it."

"So, you've read it."

I saw his eyes light up because I recognized him and his book. Yup. So, I did what any alpha woman would do while she was at work and when dealing with subordinates. "Thank you, sir. You have a nice day!" Yup, I sent him away.

He said, "It was great seeing you and even greater just to be in your presence."

My mouth hit the floor. Okay, okay, he was trying too hard. He was doing the most.

It was Friday night, and I had to rush to get to my son's football game. As I got off work and made my way through the horror of downtown Atlanta's traffic, I thought about that interaction between Clark Kent and me, and how Clark Kent's mere presence put a simple smile on my face.

I made my way south to my son's school, good ole Sandy Creek. It was tailgating time, football time, headbanging and pancake-making time. I was my son's biggest cheerleader. I went all in. Supporting my son in his athletic endeavors gave me something else to do. Football energized me. Watching my son play brought me joy and, at times, even peace. I guess you can say football was my stress release.

After a long hard week of life, I got some playtime at Friday Night Lights. I got to yell at the field, "Hit somebody! Take to the house!" or my favorite "I want some pancakes!"—all football lingo that I enjoyed.

Well, as this particular game ended, I saw someone who looked like Clark Kent from the office. I went toward him to make sure I was not just tripping, and no, it was really him.

I said, "Hey, what are you doing here?"

"My nephew plays for the other team. I wasn't sure if this was your school or not. Honestly, I knew you lived South, but I thought your son went to Creekside."

Sista E

We laughed. I asked what number was his nephew. He said thirteen. I said, "Oh, my kid was—" And as I was saying it, he said it with me. I was like, "Oh, okay."

"I remember from all the pictures hanging in your office, and I heard them announcing that name all night."

We talked as I waited on my son to come out of the locker room, but it was about the game. He knew my son's stats and plays, and we had a moment. It was a rare moment—nothing fancy, just a moment. His low-key attitude impressed me.

When my son finally came out, I turned to Clark Kent said, "It was good to see you."

"It was good to be seen." Now I know that's a pickup line. I just smiled and kept right on going.

Then Sunday came—the Lord's Day, the day of worship. I got up to go get my worship on, and who but who did I see at church? This is church y'all. I never spoke about my personal life at work. And all of a sudden, I heard, "Ms. E." I looked up because that voice sounded very familiar. I turned around, and there was Clark Kent.

"Boy, what are you doing here?"

"This is my church. I attend here, and I work in the ministry here as well. Now, what are you doing here?"

"One of my sisters asked me to come to visit. I've been hearing about Cardia Christian Fellowship Church for a while. I thought I would attend with her. But she's running late. I guess I'll just wait for her."

"Or you can come in with me, and I'll keep you company."

I smiled as he held out his arm. I took it, and we proceeded to walk into the church.

Now in my mind, I had not seen this man this much in my entire life. We had been working together for almost three years, and I had never seen him outside of the office until now, and here I had run into him twice in one weekend.

I enjoyed the service. But I mostly enjoyed seeing him. I mean, it's always a pleasure to serve and worship my God whenever I get a chance to. Fellowship with others is a plus. But this was something different, something amazing. I couldn't believe I had seen him so much, and I enjoyed it. It wasn't like it was creepy stalkerish. It was really nice to see him.

Well, let me tell you that he was a mere five foot ten but had pretty, flawless brown skin and arms swole like Debo on Friday. He had lips thick and juicy and shoes sized fourteen—definitely not my usual, not someone I would give a second look to. And he had a head full of hair—yep, hair. He had hair and wasn't my usual type. This was different.

The one thing that makes me weak in my knees is a bald man. I know, right? What is it about me and bald men? Don't act. You have your type as well. Your type may not be tall and bald like mine, but you have a type. Our type, most times, causes our legs to be weak and flop open really quick.

Now with this guy, it wasn't an immediate feeling of, *Oh, I want to go to bed with him.* He was different—more like a friend.

Monday came, and he wasn't at work. Yep, I looked for him. But he was off. The week went on, and I didn't see him until Wednesday. He walked by my office, and I called his name.

"Oh, hello, Ms. E. How are you?"

"I haven't seen you in a couple of days."

"Oh, you noticed?"

I laughed a little because he was right. I had worked with him for three years, and I had not noticed him at all before then.

"I was off Monday. I had to take my son to the doctor. And Tuesday, you were pretty busy and I kept missing you."

"Oh well, maybe I should make time for a coffee break. You should allow me to buy that coffee." I was pretty sure he knew that I knew I made more money than he did.

"Yes, you should, and you shouldn't have waited so long to ask me. Well, let's make it for tomorrow."

"Sure, we can do that."

> Sista Girl, we can't always assume someone's current position reflects their actual reality. He worked in the mailroom, and I assumed he made less than I did because I had an office and a degree. And we know the saying about assuming.

Well, our coffee break went well. We talked and talked and had a few more coffee breaks and later a dinner date. He chose the place, and I gave him my address. Remember now, before this, I had only seen him drive the company car.

He pulled up at my place ten minutes early. Of course, I wasn't ready.

> We always want other folks to be on time, but we're the late ones. I know I get it. And it's okay if I make myself late, but no one can make me late.

Anyway, he pulled up to my house in a BMW 7 Series. It was an older model, but it was clean and sharp, a pretty black, and shining. The windows were tinted just right, and it had some nice rims. Nope, this was not the work car.

We got in, and as he was opening doors for me, he got a call. We had to make a stop by his house. Look, I know what you're thinking. Oh, this is a setup. He just wanted to go by his place to create a problem so he could get a nightcap before the night started. Well, I thought that exact thing too.

He pulled up at his place and said, "Would you like to come in?"

"No, I'll wait out here for you."

"Are you sure? I'm going to only be a moment."

I wasn't falling for that trick. But he really was only a moment. He was so fast I had to ask him why we came by his place.

"I forgot my wallet."

"Oh well, you kind of need that." We laughed, and I asked, "Who else lives there with you?"

"No one but my son and me. And no, I don't live with my mom. I have full custody of my son, so there's no drama with his momma. This is my car, and it's paid in full. And my credit score—"

I laughed so loud he paused and laughed with me. That was the icebreaker for the night.

After that, the night was easy-going and amazing. It wasn't all uptight and nerve-racking. He took me to Mary Mac's. Yes, Mary Mac's, the soul food joint of the A. We laughed and talked and laughed some more. I would learn that he actually had real estate money. He owned properties all over the city. He only worked in the mailroom for medical insurance because of his son. Did I mention his son was autistic?

Wait, are y'all falling in love with this man because I surely was. He checked every box on my list. He checked boxes on a list that I never thought I wanted on a list. He went to church, he was an entrepreneur, and he was a thinker. You'd have to be a thinker to know you need a nine to five just for medical insurance for your son.

But how many of y'all know even with all that he had going for himself, he still didn't have everything he needed? He still didn't have his favor—his favor as in Proverbs 18:22.

Almost a year went by, and we became more frequent. It was now my birthday. Clark Kent brought a gift to me the night before and made me promise not to open it until I woke up. I kept my word. I didn't open it until the next morning.

It was a diamond necklace. I cried. I had told him about how my first diamond necklace, the only thing my birth father had given me that meant a lot was a gift for my high school graduation. But it was stolen. This meant so much to me. This showed me he had listened to me and was listening to me still. I was the happiest little girl in the world.

I got dressed and went to work. When I arrived, there were flowers on my desk with a note that read, "Happy birthday to the most beautiful woman I have ever met. I would love to take you to lunch today." And it was signed, "Your delivery man." The flowers were purple with a purple vase. I loved them.

He came by my office, and I thanked him. Then I said, "Yes, I'll go to lunch with you."

"Okay, be ready by one. I want to eat something light because I have big plans tonight."

"Oh?"

"Yes, I know you got your girls you're hanging with tonight, and I didn't want to sit up and obsess about you, so I made plans."

"Oh, okay then, no problem."

During lunch, he handed me a box; it was wrapped in purple wrapping paper. It was a Pandora charm bracelet. It had a football charm, a rose charm, and my birthstone charm. My mouth hung open. We ate, and when I got back to the office; another set of flowers sat on my desk. This set was white lilies, my favorite flower. I love calla lilies. I just stood there, and he was whistling as he walked on by.

This note said, "I wish you the best, and may all of your dreams come true." I texted him, "Okay, this is enough. This is too much."

He said, "Nothing is too much for a child of God. You can't tell God how and when to bless you. You just have to receive the blessings, the love."

I started to cry. No one had ever showered me with meaningful gifts, and his gifts were purposeful. His gifts were calculated and intentional. I couldn't say a word. All I could do was cry.

Now I was making a scene in the office—the office where we both worked. And up until now, people didn't know we hung out.

No, he wasn't my boyfriend—well, not officially anyway. Well, wait a minute. We talked daily, we texted daily, and we saw each other outside of the office often. We were always together. Our boys hung out. He brought his kids around me, and I brought mine around him. We went to church together, and we went out of town together. His family met me, and he met mine. But we didn't have a title; we were just friends.

I must admit, I fell weak once, and we slept together. Well, there was no sleeping. We had sex, and it was amazing. But I had given my life over to God and had become celibate. And no, not sell a bit here and sell a bit there. I had truly stopped having sex.

I grew up. I realized I couldn't sleep with every guy I met. I realized I couldn't sex my stress away. And I wanted something different. I wanted to be married and really have a man honor me and marry me, not just have sex and get nothing but a wet pussy. I found out I could wet my own pussy with a lot less of a headache.

But I broke my vow with him and felt so bad. He vowed he would not allow me to do that again. He saw how heartbroken I was over that. He didn't pressure me. I chose to sleep with him.

I was having a really, really bad time. My friend had died, and I was heartbroken. Then one thing led to another.

> How many of you know one thing doesn't lead to another unless someone is leading? It's always purposeful.

We never had sex again, and we never even came close to having sex again. Now I am not going to lie; that was the hardest thing in the world. But we were intentional about where we went and what we watched. We didn't want anything to add more pressure on us and tempt us again.

Now, after all of these flower deliveries, I was standing there, crying after lunch, and he was standing there with a look of pride and a huge smile on his face. So, people started adding things up.

I took my lilies home with me. I figured one set of flowers at work and one set at home. And I actually got off work at a decent hour. On my way home, one of my friends called to say happy birthday and that she, unfortunately, had to cancel our plans for tonight.

I got home and got ready to go out, wearing my classic catch-a-man black dress with spaghetti strings. I was looking good. I already had my hair done, and the one friend who couldn't go out said she had ordered me a makeup artist to come over to do my makeup. As I was getting my makeup done, my other friend called and said her car broke down and she couldn't make it tonight either. Now I was sitting here, all dressed up with nowhere to go, and it was my birthday. I pitched a fit. I was definitely in my feelings.

I called my girls and fussed at them, then said to myself, "I'm going out anyway. Forget them." I was not going to be all dolled up with no place to go.

Clark Kent had already made his separate plans with his friends, so calling him wasn't even a consideration. Besides, he kind of spent the whole day with me, and he had already given me gifts. I wouldn't swing my attitude his way. But my girls leaving me hanging, oh, the nerve of them.

I opened my door, and there was a black Rolls-Royce limo sitting in front of my house. I was like, "Who done left their car at my front door?" I looked around and saw this not-so-tall man standing there with flowers in his hand, wearing a black suit. I love a classic black suit well-fitted on any man, and even more on one I'm attracted to.

I heard vague music playing in the background. I looked over, and it was Clark Kent standing there. I was in total shock and amazement. "What are you doing here?"

In a smooth operator voice, he said, "Where else would I be than with the love of my life?"

I just stood there. My mouth wasn't hanging open, but that's because the lip gloss that was matted on my lips was stuck together.

I thought I was just thinking this, but apparently, I said out loud, "You have never said you love me, and I'm pretty sure you never called me the love of your life."

"Have I ever lied to you?"

I laughed, and something started running down my face. Some may say it was tears, but I think someone was cutting onions around me. "I thought you had major plans tonight. What are you doing here?"

"Well, good thing your girls canceled on you."

"Right, it is." Now, in my mind, I was thinking I didn't remember telling him the girls canceled on me, but I was just so excited that I didn't care to think too hard.

He said, "Well, my dear, your chariot awaits," as he opened the door to the limo. How could I resist?

Inside he had a dozen long-stemmed red roses waiting for me. I smelled them and said, "Thank you, my dear." He was smiling, and I was crying. In the background, I heard Anita Baker's "Lead Me into Love." Now, if you know like I know, if he put on some Anita Baker, he's getting them drawls without any hesitation. When Anita sings her love songs, and you already have feelings for that person, well, that's just baby-making music. I am in love with everything Anita has ever sung. But I was still sitting there in shock, and thinking, *no, he can't possibly remember Anita Baker is my favorite artist.*

He said, "I want you to listen to this song I picked out just for you, just for tonight." I listened and thought, *wow, he remembers. Wow, he's paying attention to me.* I believe we talked about music maybe on the first date. And this was now almost a year later.

When a woman is loved correctly, properly, you will get the best outta her. I felt like a queen, like I was royalty.

We pulled up at the Sun Dial Restaurant. Now Atlanta's Sun Dial Restaurant is kinda like a trademark in Atlanta. It stands about 723 feet up in the air on Peachtree Street and has a three-hundred-sixty-degree panoramic view of Atlanta's skyline. You don't move out of your seat to enjoy it either as the room slowly spins you around to view the city from way up in the air. It is the most beautiful you will ever see.

We got there, and the door person said, "Happy Birthday, Ms. Emori." Then the waitress said, "Happy Birthday, Ms. Emori. Your table is awaiting you."

We entered a private area, and there were all of my girls who had bailed on me. We laughed, and I cried so hard. I was like, "These heffas dipped on me at the last minute." Well, I'm sure you guessed it by now; they were part of the setup. He had called them early on and told them to make plans and cancel on me the day of.

After greeting everyone, we ate. We all had the same or similar food items, and it was delicious. Toward the middle, Mr. Clark Kent made a toast and thanked everyone for getting me good and upset. We all laughed because I was truly upset. Or had been.

He then gave this speech about "It doesn't take all day to recognize sunshine. Either the sun is out, or it's a cloudy, rainy day.

Either way, you can immediately spot it." And I had no clue where he was going with his story. Then he said to me as he walked around the table toward me, "Emori, I knew from the moment I met you that you were the one. And seeing you three times in a weekend was my confirmation. You kept appearing at the same places I frequently attend, work, football, and church. I knew you were the woman for me. Emori, will you do me the honor and be my wife?"

He opened this box with this really beautiful but small ring. The diamond was so small against my fat fingers that you could barely tell it was a diamond. I swear it looked like it came out of the crackerjack box.

You best be believing—well, once the shock and awe wore off—I screamed, "Yes!" I quickly put his really small ring on my finger without hesitation. I knew better than to say something about this tiny diamond. But it could have been all he could afford. I mean, after all, he was a single dad. But let's be honest. He could have given me a piece of newspaper and made it into a ring, and I would have still screamed "Yes," and I wore it proudly!

> Sista Gal, why do we get so caught up in the big fairytale ring, the big wedding with lots of people, spending too much money, and still don't own property? Why do we allow the media and entertainment industry to dictate what we should view as success or what we view as happy? It's not the size of his ring that matters; it's the size of his heart that matters—and shoe size if

you're anything like me because, let's be honest, sex matters.

I didn't know this man but right at a year. I had two boys, both with barely part-time daddies. And here, this man whom technically I was never even in a relationship with—well, we never said we were in an exclusive relationship, although we spent days and nights with each other, and we had only had sex once in that year—asking me to marry him.

Yeah, maybe that's it. I said yes because I was horny. I hadn't had sex in two years before him. I was focused on myself, and let's be honest, to go without sex after you've already been introduced to it after you're already a born freak, and just go cold turkey because you're tired of all the jive turkeys is nothing to sneeze at. So yeah, maybe I said yes so fast because I was horny and ready to get my freak on again, except in a legal way. Because, clearly, me saying yes after the day this man just gave me played no clue in my decision. Nor did the fact he had developed a relationship with my fatherless sons have anything to do with me. No, that couldn't be it.

It had nothing to do with how he honored and loved me or how he pursued me even before I knew he was pursuing me. He found me while I was working—yup, definitely Proverbs 18:22. And it definitely wasn't because he purposely didn't give us a title because he had plans for us in the long run. He was really on those proverbs that reminded him we were friends until we were wed.

He sealed the night with "You are my favor." And I sealed the night talking to God about how He showed out on me. He sent me this man who was right under my nose. But because Clark Kent wasn't six foot four, bald, and wearing a uniform, I didn't even notice him—well, until God smacked me in my face with him. I had not noticed the Clark Kent right in front of me. I was too caught up in his looks and my typical type.

> How many of us believe we are the prize that God sent to man to be his helpmate, not beneath him, not above him, but by his side? You ever wonder why God took his rib to create us, womenfolk? Because that is where he wanted us, standing by his side always and forever. God could have taken a bone from a man's foot or a piece of his brain, but no, he took a rib. Think about that.
>
> God had formed this whole world, and still, it wasn't complete for him to rest until he created a woman. Yes, we can indeed be his beautiful dream or his worst nightmare. According to Genesis, the Bible says he called her "bone of my bones, flesh of my flesh." The purpose of the woman being created was to help her mate. But if you notice, she was his mate before she started helping. It wasn't until God created her did she become his help. Therefore, man must know and love himself before he can know and love you. If he is still lost in the wilderness,

he can't lead you, guide you, or love you.
He just can't!

Don't just accept a proposal. Know what His vision is. Know where that man is headed in his life. Know what his values are. But most of all, know where his heart is. Is his heart tucked away in the same place your heart is, like in God? Ask him what he is proposing to do.

We have to allow God to make a man outta him before we try to make him our husband.

CHAPTER 12

Exhale Him, Inhale You, Breathe

Sista Girl, can we talk? I mean, really talk, upfront, open, and honest? No, not more stories, just some real girl talk.

If you noticed, some of the stories in this book didn't really have endings. The endings were vague and not solidified. Why? Because we believed what they taught us.

To get over a man, you get under another. Yup, we were taught there are plenty of fish in the sea or don't cry over spilled milk. Get a rag, wipe it up, and move along. Yup, pretty much just move right on along and take all that baggage from one situation to the next, building deeper strongholds. This is what we were taught. Or take the old-fashioned saying, "It is better to have a piece of a man than none at all."

No, Sista Gal. It is better to have *peace* than *pieces* of a man. So, let's figure out how we allowed ourselves to get here.

You're crying and upset at a man who was never yours. He never said, "It's me and you, baby. I'm yours, and you're mine. Will you be?" What he said was, "Let's not put any titles on it, and let's just do what we do." And in your head, you said, "Oh, I can change his mind," and flopped yo legs open.

Put yo good dental work on his genitals!

What you thought was, "My pussy is pure gold, and I can get him to commit. I can ride him into submission." You thought you had that I'm-calling-my-momma kind of sunshine pussy. Yup, nope. What he said was what he meant. He just wanted your goods, and you heard whatcha wanted to hear.

No, no, Sista Girl. Pick up your face.

I know you thought you had that platinum pussy, but she had the deep throat magic. Oh, excuse me, were you offended again? Well, this here is some grown folks talking.

He said what he meant, and his actions followed. You just walked in what you wanted, so your heart followed. You got emotionally involved, and yup, you fell in love while he fell in bed.

Stop it, Sis. You saw the signs. Your womanly intuition notified you that something ain't right. If he is out with friends and never answers your calls, if your name is not in his phone or it's your kid's name in his phone instead of yours, yup, nope, you're not the one.

If your name's not Emori or Wife with ICE—in case of emergency—behind it, yeah, nope, he's just not that into you, boo.

The famous quote "Men lie," yeah, they do. But we convince ourselves with what we want and not what he said and what his actions are.

He loved you for that moment, and he enjoyed every moment. Maybe y'all even went out in public a few times, and maybe he returned a call or two. But, Sista Girl, he never committed to you. You turned this into what your heart wanted and what you really deserved. However, what you got was his truth. He's just not that into you.

You got a broken heart because you found out he was with another chick or had another baby with someone else or the ultimate, he married her and not you. But did he ever commit to you, or did he just use you?

Maybe he did say, "Baby, you're the one," with his words, but his actions didn't follow. Maybe he proposed to you, but what did he propose?

Even if you married him, you had clues, and your intuition knew something wasn't quite right. But because he paid the bills, you allowed him to get away with murder and with unanswered questions.

So, Sis, Let's talk.

You ever use the toilet to go number two, and before you flush, you look? You evaluate it like it's brown, it's green, it's big, or you say, "All that pushing for those little bitty ones?" Come on, let's be real with each other.

> The doctors recommend that you actually do look back and analyze before you flush. How else can you tell the doctor what's going on in your insides? It's healthy to do it.

But it's the same concept. You do this when you continue to look back at the brokenness, the hurt, and the pain of the last situation. Yup, you're analyzing *your shit*. Stop doing that. This is not healthy for you.

You dodged a bullet. This fool is crazy, but you can't see that because you're getting dicked down. You can't see how mentally challenged this man really is. And yet, we're crying and boo-hooin' over this man.

I saw my Mr. Bus Driver some years later. I saw what he turned into. Wait. He might have always been that, but I was too busy riding that good dick to see it. And I was upset at myself. I was crying and depressed and going through all kinds of changes over this man. But after seeing him years later, I wanted my tears back. All of them.

So, check your feelings, boo, because nobody cares about what you feel. Feelings aren't facts. Get out of your feelings, and get into your Bible. Get into the motion, and get into action. Realize your feelings change with the weather. You need some consistency, and you need some healing.

Oh, you mad? Oh, you're big mad, huh? But you broke your own heart, sweetheart. You stayed too long and went too far.

Now let's heal. It's time to let go.

Get into some scriptures and start your healing. See how the stories relate to your life.

Here are some scriptures for you and my interpretation of **Ephesians 4**.

> Therefore, putting away lying *[he lied to you, you lied to you]*. Let each one of you speak the truth with his neighbor, for we are members of one another. *[Now it's time to stop lying to yourself and speak the truth to you. Speak your truth to him]*. Be angry, and do not sin. *[Yup, it happened. Be mad, big mad; cry; and scream. Let it out.]* Do not let the sun go down on your wrath *[but don't stay mad, get up from there]* nor give place to the devil. *[The longer you stay mad and hurt, the easier you give him and the devil permission to keep hurting you]*. Let him who stole steal no longer *[he can't have your*

joy, your peace, your destiny any longer]. But rather let him labor, working with his hands what is good that he may have something to give him who has need. *[Allow God to avenge you with that man. God can get him better than you can. Don't waste any more energy on what has already happened.]* Let no corrupt word proceed out of your mouth *[speak to him no longer with pain in your voice]* but what is good for necessary edification *[if you have children with this man, no longer speak with pain to him or about him]* that it may impart grace to the hearers. Let all bitterness, wrath, anger, clamor, and evil-speaking be put away from you with all malice. *[It's time to heal you, and it's time to heal your heart]*. (Ephesians 4:23–32)

Remember the scripture that goes something like, "Let your heart not be troubled. Ye believe in me also believe." You deserve peace, love, and happiness. Hell, sex is optional. Well, maybe not exactly like that. But there are toys that will give you a thrill with a lot fewer headaches.

In Psalm 34:4, the Word says: "I sought the Lord, and He heard me and delivered me from all my fears." You have to be intentional about your healing. Be purposeful about living, dreaming, and laughing.

It's a fine line between faith and foolery. A well-known Atlanta pastor once said, "To change your life, change your HAT, meaning change your *habits*, change your *associations*, change your *thoughts*."

You ask, "How do I get up from here?" Well, here's a start. Just do it. Just do it! Don't talk about it; be about it. Just do it! Take one step, then another, and then another until you see the progress.

The **habits** are the men you repeatedly date, fall in lust with, or have sex with. You wonder why you keep dating the same kind of guy or your type. It is a habit. You haven't healed you enough to recognize the same hurts, habits, and hang-ups that exist in the next person. Until you heal, you'll keep attracting the same kind of man.

Your **associations**—you're pissed off, your BFF is miserable, your other friend got a divorce, and now all of y'all are sitting up and male-bashing. And here you got an amen corner to the foolery. No, get with some healed folks or some folks trying to heal. Trying to be better and not those who are stuck and enjoying the misery. Halfway friends talk about yesterday. They're stuck there.

Change your **thoughts**. Clear your head of all the negative things and thoughts you have. If someone comes to you with drama or misery, stop them in their tracks, and change the subject on purpose.

Just like you are what you eat, your mind is what you feed it. Get you an accountability partner, a covenant partner who can handle the change. That's going through the process with you.

There comes a time in a woman's life where she has to grab her balls and boss up. You have no time for pity parties. No time for woe is me. Oh, he did this, and he ain't do that. And wham, wham, wham!

Girl, you need to stop it. I'm not telling you it didn't happen. I'm not telling you it doesn't hurt. What I am telling you is to get up from here.

Well, how, you ask? Great question. Church folks always tell you what you need to do but not how to do it.

Did you know that the most dangerous creature on earth is a woman? She can destroy a king and a kingdom in a swift of an eye. Only smart men know how powerful women are. Do you know how powerful you are?

You are the prize. It is a privilege to date you, to marry you. God is a God of purpose. In the Bible, God was about done creating things—you know, things like the world. I imagine He looked around and was like, "Wow, I do good work." He was popping His collar and patting Himself on the back.

And then the Holy Spirit was like, "Nah, bruh, something is missing, although I can't quite put my finger on it. We've done great work, but Adam is a man. He can't do it all on his own."

God was like, "Yeah, you're right. Let me get him some help. I'll make him a helpmate, one who will help him." God had already created everything else, so when He created a woman, He said, "Okay, she can handle things from here. I can go be God."

God created women for a specific course. Now to find that course, that purpose, you must go to the one who created you. Go to the Father God to find a meaningful purpose for your life. He installed all of us with gifts and passions.

A famous person once said, "You can have more degrees than a thermometer, but if you don't have a purpose, you don't have anything."

Exhale Him, Inhale You, Breathe

Don't let this mess fool you. There is going to be a progress after this mess. You just have to do your part and get through the difficult times.

What do you do when your head and heart disagree? When your heart is caught up on the "It's possible," but your head is on the reality of "This nut is crazy?"

I know sometimes we love a man to our soul. But sometimes, if that love isn't reciprocated, we must turn the corner, make the switch, get outta our own way, and get to *better*.

I know you want to have faith to believe he's going to change. But no, Sis, he's not. I know you serve him, well, riding that surfboard and all. But he is not going to change. Not until he is ready to change, and even then, his change has nothing to do with you. That's between him and his God.

That's his journey, Sis. Now go take yours.

CHAPTER 13

Heal With Courage, Strength, & Wisdom

Wait. Before we continue, get yourself by a window or sit outside and feel the fresh air. Turn your phone off for a moment. Grab something cold to drink.

You got it? You're there? Okay, now, let's take a deep breath. Inhale, exhale, breathe again. Open your mind, open your heart, and open your spirit. Now let's do the work.

It wasn't that she was changing. It was that she was finally becoming herself. It's time to become you—the you God created you to become. Here's how.

- Get some paper or make a note on your phone. Either way, write it down. Every single detail that your heart remembers, all the embarrassing details, all the hurtful details, all the yeah-that-just-happened-to-me details—write it down. Read it, and write down more.

- Acknowledge that this all just happened to you. Yes, baby girl, it happened. It really happened.

- Read it again. Now cry, scream, feel it—every hurt, every disappointment, every but-our-future moment, every my-baby-won't. Feel it, all of it.

- Now burn it. Burn that piece of paper, burn the notebook. If it's on your phone or computer or tablet, delete it. Just get rid of it. Get rid of it, so it's not returning.

- Now, pull out more paper, write the vision, and make it plain. God gave you dreams, passion, and gifts. Now is the time to use them.

- Pour into yourself. Get yourself some affirmations. Stuff like scriptures and use them as affirmations. Speak God's words back to you: "I am fearfully and wonderfully made. I am beautiful. I am healing. I deserve happiness. I am becoming. I am healthy. God loves me. I am the light of his Word." Read it, write it, and speak it daily and hourly. Every time you have a relapse and remember what happened, pull out your affirmations and affirm yourself with love. Your love, Jesus's love—read those affirmations back to you so you can see what God said. Write them so they will be a repetition in your mind and become new memories. And most of all, speak it out loud so you can then hear what you said to yourself. And know that no matter what you've done, you deserve better.

- Now here's a step many tend to forget because some people think it's not important or they haven't accepted it. But this is the biggest step of them all. Are you ready? Are you listening? Come close, and pay attention. *Forgive yourself.* You saw the signs, you read the clues, and your womanly intuition kicked it. More importantly, you played a part in it. Remember that time you said, "I ain't stupid?" I know you did. You allowed it. Now it's time to own it. Release it. Forgive it.

Until you do something different, nothing will ever change. It's like if you're standing around and your nose starts bleeding, are you going to stand there, or are you going to go make it stop bleeding? You do something to get it to stop. Right? That is exactly what must be done. You have to do something different to get something different.

Philippians 3:13 tells us to forget the things behind and press our way forward.

Someone once said, "You can't turn everyone into a believer, but you can make them a witness. Keep working on yourself."

As stated in the Bible, "To everything there is a season and a time to every purpose under the heaven." Ecclesiastes 3:7 states, "A time to kill, and a time to heal; a time to break down, and a time to build up. A time to weep and a time to laugh; a time to mourn, and a time to dance."

Sis, it's time to heal, it's time to laugh, and it's time to dance.

Sometimes the smallest step in the right direction ends up being the biggest step in your life. Tiptoe if you must, but take the step.

Read Psalms 37 and 7. Quiet down before God, and be prayerful before Him. Now take a deep breath. Exhale.

Then say this, "Everything I am not made me everything I am."

- Make do with what you have.
- Be thankful.
- Do what you love to do.
- Enjoy the simple pleasures of life.
- Just believe.
- Remember, you are not any further because you don't have focus.

You can't win divided among yourself. Say this out loud, "I am fire when I am focused."

- Focus.
- Find your reason.
- Own your mind.
- Concentrate on your task.
- Understand your distractions.
- See the big picture.
- Stay focused!

CHAPTER 14

Finish Strong: Sing, Sing, Celebrate

Celebrate *you* as much as possible! No one but you and God know what you've grown through. No one can tell your story as you can. So, every chance you get to celebrate you, go ahead and celebrate! Celebrate your birthday. Celebrate the day you lose five pounds. Celebrate the day your pity party ends. Celebrate loving you! Sing loudly, off-key, on me. Sing it, boo.

You deserve it. You're raising your babies. Celebrate, not complain. Celebrate your baby. You did that.

Go back to school. Start a new career. Find your passion. Look through the windshield of life, not the rearview mirror of it. Life is moving fast, and to keep up, you have to move and adjust.

Get healed before your brokenness breaks someone else. Too many people want to get to the end results and skip the process. The enemy is after your mind. If he can get your mind, the rest of the body will follow.

If it's over, get over it. You deserve better than the brokenness of your past. But if you don't believe that in your head and your heart, then changing for the better will never happen. Either you win, or you learn, but you should never miss out.

You're trying to make things happen instead of letting them happen. That's control. Release your need to control what happens next. Allow God to be the head of your life. It's never too late to begin again, to start over, to start anew. If you're breathing, then live. It's your life; own it.

Finish Strong: Sing, Sing, Celebrate

Don't rehearse it, *renurse* or replay the pain of yesterday. Yesterday has passed away. Let it die. And what do we do when something has died? We bury it. Quit trying to climb that mountain and speak to it. Every time you open your mouth, you give birth to your words. So sing it, Sis!

Think of it like this. You fell and scraped your leg, and it's bleeding a lot. It hurts, it looks bad, but you managed to stop the bleeding, and as time goes on, it stops hurting. It's healing, but you can still see the bruises. Then a scab starts to grow; that definitely means it's healing. Someone asked you what happened to your leg, and now you're reliving it. You're remembering it, and that alone is enough to bring back the pain. That's renursing it.

Now you're home, and you're looking at it. You're picking at the scab again—that's replaying it—and picking and picking. Next thing you know, it's bleeding all over again.

Darn it. Now, you have to start the healing process all over again.

This is what we do with our emotional scars. The more we relive and talk about what happened, the more we reopen those scars. That's you picking at the scab on the sore again. And we know the skin can't regrow if you keep exposing it to the air. The air is giving it life again.

Stop giving life to that hurt, that grief. Live again.

Let's change your atmosphere. Let's change your thought process, and let's heal your soul and make you whole again.

Get some different music to listen to. Get some inspirational movies and music to feed your soul. Read a new book, start a new class, and learn a new recipe. Find yourself, and chase after yourself. Everything you were giving and pouring into him, do it for you, boo. Get your life off layaway, Sis. It's time to live your best life.

We have to watch what we put into our souls. So, how do things enter into our souls? I am so glad you asked. Things can enter our soul through our eyes with what we see. They can enter through our nose with what we smell like colognes, candles, funk... We all know how a scent can bring about a memory. It can enter our soul through our mouth in what we say or what is said to us, and that leads to our ears.

And last but not least is our vagina. When that man enters your body with his penis, he's releasing into your soul. Stop trusting sex to heal your broken heart. Sista Girl, it's time we guard up our soul. It's time we protect our souls like never before. It's a matter of life and death—our lives or our death, your life or your death.

We are the sum of the choices we've made. We are responsible for what we do and how we respond to what happened to us. Stop being the victim.

Remember, sometimes the smile we longed to get is too expensive. You can't have the strength and not have sorrow. Had it not been so painful, you wouldn't have found your strength.

Repeat this to yourself: When you have been conditioned to think like a chicken, you can't soar like an eagle.

Quit trying to climb that mountain and speak to it. Every time you open your mouth, you're giving birth to your words. Did you know you can hear your own words with your own ears?

Stop being addicted to pain. There is no badge of honor for saying over and over to yourself that he hurt you or what you experienced. By doing this, I believe we allow our minds to be the source of our misery. So, let's change things around. Let's start pursuing purpose. Start figuring out your greatness.

Heal from the inside, and it will show on the outside. And the right healed man will see you. Remember Ruth was working in the field when Boaz saw her.

And for the record, Clark Kent turned into my Superman again at the altar when we said, "I do." At that time, he upgraded my ring from a .10 karat to a 2.5 karat white bling that sits on my finger from my Superman.

Remember the scripture "If you're faithful over a few things?" Well, he wanted to see if I was loyal to him or his money.

So, I'll leave this scripture for you, Romans 12:21 (KJV): "Do not be overcome by evil, but overcome evil with good." My interpretation of this scripture is let the past pass away and start doing good for yourself. As in Romans 12:2, Old things have passed away all things are become NEW.

LOVE TOKENS

Sista Girl, take what you need from this book, and leave the rest. Allow God to be the center of your life and soar into greatness. You are breathing, so go live. Don't allow the past to hold you back anymore. You can't wear a crown with your head down.

I believe if we can heal our women, we can heal our land. It is with her honey that's sweet—sweet enough to calm the beast. Remember, it always seems impossible until it's done. And remember, too, life and death are in the power of your tongue. Watch what you tell yourself! Believe in God. Believe in yourself. Believe you can begin again. From this day forward, don't let anyone tell you or make you feel less than what you really are.

CLOSING PRAYER

Heavenly Father, thank you for the doors you've closed. Thank you for the mountains I had to climb. Thank you for never leaving me, even when I wanted to leave myself. Thank you for the growing pains, and thank you for loving me past the pain. Thank you for loving me in spite of me. Now Father God, as I begin this new journey of loving me, I thank you in advance for my healing. I thank you for your grace that allows me to grow from broken to blossoming. All these things I ask in Jesus's name. Amen.

Now grow through what you're going through...

ABOUT THE AUTHOR

Sista E is the founder of DreamGirl Empowerment Group LLC, a humanitarian organization seeking to help women find and fulfill their God-given purpose. Inspired by her life experiences, she became a certified Parent & Life Consultant and mentor, guiding lives in her community. Sista E is also an inspirational speaker, appearing at numerous functions as the mistress of ceremonies, where she has earned a reputation for making every event memorable.

Sista E's core message is from Colossians 4–6 (AMP), "Let your speech at all times be gracious and pleasant, seasoned with salt, so that you will know how to answer each one."

She is a writer whose work is a classic example of art imitating life. Her witty responses, love of Christ, and servant's heart keep people wanting more from her. She can give her readers an in-depth look into the lives of her characters as she brings them to life. Inspired by her life experiences, Sista E offers her readers hope at the end of an arduous journey.

Being the daughter of preacher parents, a miracle child counted as dead until God said she would live, she has lived through heartbreaks, regrets, and questionable decisions. Sista E is the mother of two amazing young men, and she is their biggest cheerleader, encouraging them to follow their dreams while turning their obstacles into opportunities.

She is also a member of Tau Alpha Delta Christian Sorority, Inc. and an Alumnus of Morris Brown College in Atlanta, GA.

Sista E has a Podcast called Conversations with Sista E discussing life, love and propserity.

To connect with Sista E, please visit her website at https://SistaE.Chat

CPSIA information can be obtained
at www.ICGtesting.com
Printed in the USA
LVHW041942140723
752117LV00003B/411

9 781638 601364